THE GOOD ITALIAN GIRL

My Personal Story of Awakening and
Redefining the Cultural Rules as an
Australian-Italian Woman

By Claudia Callisto

The Good Italian Girl

First Edition 2021
Copyright © 2021 Claudia Callisto

All rights reserved. No part of this publication may be reproduced, stored in a retrieval system, or transmitted in any form or by any means, electronic, mechanical, photocopying, recording or otherwise, without the prior written permission from both the copyright owner and publisher.

Disclaimer

This story is about my own personal experiences and my thoughts and analysis regarding how I grew up in Adelaide, Australia, within my Italian family and cultural community. All the information, techniques, skills, and concepts contained within this publication are of the nature of general comment only and are not in any way recommended as individual advice. The intent is to offer a variety of information to provide a wider range of choices now and in the future, recognising that we all have widely diverse circumstances and viewpoints. Should any reader choose to make use of the information contained herein, this is their decision and the author and publishers do not assume any responsibilities whatsoever under any condition or circumstances.

ISBN: 978-0-6489958-3-8 (Paperback)

For more information about the author, Claudia Callisto, speaking engagements, or media enquiries, please visit: www.shininglightcd.com.au or email: claudiacallisto@optusnet.com.au

Publishing Coach: Emma Hamlin, Change Maker Press PTY LTD
Publishing Partnership with Change Maker Press
www.changemakerpress.com.au

Editor: Kate Boccaccio

IT'S TIME TO CELEBRATE!

Let's take action now, my fellow ethnic soul sisters, and start embracing a new chapter in our lives!

Download Your Free 'Live Your Best Life' Journal

As a way of saying thank you for purchasing a copy of The Good Italian Girl, I'm gifting you a free journal you can download! It's an exclusive bonus for readers of my book, so what are you waiting for?

Stop putting your life on hold.

Live it now! You'll uncover how to document your unique story, family traditions, and family messages for your own legacy. Download here:

www.shininglightcd.com.au

Let's shine brightly together!

Join my VIP Facebook group:

The Good Italian Girl and Giussa

Let's connect with other ethnic soul sisters at network group meetings and special events

Connect with Claudia Callisto at:

www.shininglightcd.com.au
Facebook.com/Shining Light.cd
Instagram @Shininglight.cd
Instagram @claudiacallisto
Email: claudiacallisto@optusnet.com.au

Contents

Prologue 1
PART ONE 11
Where My Giussa Life Began 13
Growing Up and My Mother's Influence 15
The Giussa Road Block and Turning Point 37
Meeting Other Giussa Ethnic Chicks at University.. 44
Going Out Giussa Style 49
Meeting Your Future Partner: An Australian-Italian Boy 54
The Ethnic Courtship Travel Rules 58
Getting Married to an Australian-Italian Boy 64
Being Accepted by Your Future Husband's Family 70
Infertility and Being an Ethnic Woman 82
The Ethnic Girls' Career Options 87
PART TWO 107
Our Italian Traditions 109
The Old Italy, the New Italy and the Australian-Italians 114
Ethnic Children Are Loved Deeply 120
Ethnic Respect 127
Ethnic Values 129
Keeping the Ethnic Traditions 133
Doing the Ethnic Visits 135
Christmas Day 138

Italians and Money... 139
PART THREE **141**
Changing the Narrative for the Next Generation: Hopes for My Child 143
What Our Children Want From Us as Ethnic Raised Parents 144
Changing the Rules for Our Children's Wellbeing................................... 148
What Do We Want to Pass On to Our Children?..................................... 150
Our Ethnic Family – Redefined by Our Generation 158
PART FOUR **161**
Consequences of the Ethnic Rule Book... 163
What Is the Cost of These Obligations?... 169
Competitive Women 176
Still a Proud Giussa Today 178
PART FIVE **181**
Evolving: Embracing a New Chapter 183
The Start Of My Transformation.. 186
Kaleidoscopes... 188
Establishing My New Business Shining Light... 190
Death, Italians and Regrets.. 193
How Have I Personally Redefined the Unwritten Italian Rule Book?..... 204
What Is the "Ethnic Soul Sister Connection?".. 209
Discovering the Magic of Journaling and Positive Affirmations............ 214
Why Write a Book About Being a Good Italian Girl and Giussa?.......... 217
What is My Personal Legacy? 219
Dare to Dream... 223
Epilogue.. 226

Prologue

"Girl, you have your mother's life," was my dreaded realisation today while napping on the couch. It is Sunday afternoon, and I am currently having a quick power nap on the couch before I face the next couple of hours sorting out that never-ending basket of weekly clothes to fold and iron.

Then maybe a quick coffee and onto tonight's meal preparation before the hubby and my child come and ask for dinner options. There is no quick toasted cheese sandwich for my family! Oh no, I'm feeding ethnics, people! It is only rustic Italian food for them. Maybe a bit of braciola ragu, or they might be happy tonight with a quick spaghettata all'olio. No UBER eats in my family.

Omg, maybe I could develop a business called Ethnic UBER eats … hmm, put that entrepreneurial brain away, Claudia. You don't have the time to dream and you were not born to be an entrepreneur. You're an ethnic chick with domestic obligations, that's a boys' role.

Yes, I have definitely turned into my mother and her life with my dad. I said that would never happen to me.

At the age of 17 I was determined I wasn't going to simply be a Good Italian Girl and Giussa chick. I was going to be a Good Italian

Girl and Giussa with a corporate career, big financial ambitions and have lots of adventure and travel in my life. I was going to achieve it all and tick off all those bucket list dreams I had, along with getting married and having a big Italian family and doing all that other stuff I was pre-programmed and expected to do.

Yes, I was secretly dreaming big. Bigger than my parents' expectations of me. Bigger than what good Australian-Italian girls were expected to be. I was going to achieve things in my life: do things, go places and see the world. I was going to be everything I wanted to be and no one was going to say I could not do this or that because my family and culture expected me to follow the unwritten cultural rules.

I was going to be a Giussa on steroids: "Watch me achieve my dreams, world!" I would tell myself.

So, what happened? Exhaustion happened. Too many ethnic expectations on myself and from others. Too much focus on being perfect and there for everyone but myself. No time for real fun or adventurous interests. The only time available for the grind of our ethnic life: work, home, kids … you know the drill.

Hey fellow ethnic chicks, do you feel the same?

When you're on the brink of exhaustion, and you don't feel like yourself anymore. You're no longer reaching your true potential, and you feel like your world is constantly spinning around you with more and more jobs to do and more and more family expectations to meet. You simply feel like it is never enough, no matter what you do or how hard you work.

I don't mean spinning like in those step classes you mastered and the grapevine you loved doing in your heyday 80's aerobic classes kitted out in your sexy lycra. No, I mean you're spinning with overwhelm, lacking in energy, drowning in stress, and disconnected from your life dreams. The person you once were, hanging out with those Giussa besties you used to giggle, dream and have fun with, feels like a distant memory.

Imagine what it would be like to calm the chaos down in our lives, recalibrate, re-energise and live our best lives, free of cultural expectations.

Firstly, let me explain the word "Giussa" and the expression "ethnic chick"

These expressions are not intended to be racist or discriminatory. They are terms I use in conversation with my fellow ethnic girlfriends. We relate to these terms and connect to them from a place deep within our soul. We are not being judgemental. It is not a negative label and it is not condescending. It just describes our environment, our alter ego, our own internal label for ourselves. We will sometimes call a friend a Giussa in a joking manner, but never as a put-down.

I am a proud ethnic chick, and I am proud to call myself a Giussa. I am my own version of an Italian Giussa. Everyone has their own version, and no version is the same. We are all unique and I feel a sense of power and confidence being a Giussa.

This reference - in the context of this book - means a good Italian raised girl in the 1980's mainly: we were all Giussas even though we were not named Giussepina. We were girls raised by strict parents and we followed their rules and the cultural expectations. We worked hard and were very respectful. We dreamed of marrying the man of our dreams and living happily ever after with our own family of children and being part of our big ethnic community.

By labelling myself as a Giussa, or ethnic chick, I am actually identifying myself as a female immigrant child who grew up with strict family values and rules. We essentially follow what I call the 'ethnic cultural rule book'. This book has never been published. It is handed down the generations verbally and enforced using 'the look' and harsh words spoken by our mothers, fathers, brothers, grandparents, relatives and the ethnic community surrounding us. These cultural expectations mean that my role and responsibility within my immediate family would focus on not only working a job/career but also cooking, cleaning, shopping, looking after my child and husband's needs. In addition to my immediate family, it means also helping my ageing parents and parent-in-laws, siblings and other family members. If I then had any time left, I would try and pursue some personal time and connections with friends and that ever-elusive regular exercise routine and healthy eating habits I needed to implement.

I believe that my upbringing within a culturally orientated environment has made me unique in terms of my perception towards life, other individuals and how I think, feel, work and live in this world. I am a funny, smart and kind-hearted person who likes to try new things and empower others. This is my own personal version of the definition of Giussa. It's a feeling of being soul connected to other like-minded individuals from an ethnic background who just 'get' me - the real me - and with whom I can be my true ethnic influenced self around, without having to explain my actions or thoughts. I can talk how I want to talk and not be judged. I can simply relax and have fun and essentially not feel judged for how I was brought up, how I behave and how I express myself. In fact I felt that my culture provided more depth to my life and having the ability to converse in more than one language was a skill, in my view.

My definition of Giussa is one that is positive: it is a fun and innocent reference. It connects me to my soul sisters growing up. I am connected to an era where the world was embracing change. I was an ambitious ethnic girl determined to fulfil her career dreams and I was filled with hope that things would change for me.

In the 1980's I loved my high hair, black eyeliner, my wardrobe of black 80's clothes and short skirts, my shoulder pads in my suits just like Madonna, and my wide-waisted belt sitting just below my hips, styled just right with my large, unique earrings. I loved to dance to 80's music and laugh with my fellow Giussa and Mario friends. I loved my look, and I thought I was pretty hot-looking and stylish. I wore the Giussa label with a sense of pride.

However, I am aware that for many ethnic females, this term was also used in a discriminatory manner - especially at school - and represented something to them that made them feel isolated and different from other more Anglo girls. Being ethnic was not something they wanted to be labelled as. They did not want to stand out in their class or amongst their peers, and to be called a Giussa was offensive to them.

Not all ethnic females use this term and I wish to acknowledge that up front. I apologise if you are offended by my wording within this book, as this is not my intention. Nor is it my intention to insult my Italian heritage or my cultural community. I am a proud member of this community in Australia.

I am writing this book about my journey and the thought of trying to change the words Giussa and ethnic chick to be more politically correct just doesn't give my message or story justice or read in the same context.

I acknowledge that I am actually allowed to call *myself* an ethnic chick and Giussa and it's a phrase I regularly use to explain my reasoning or my actions or sometimes to simply laugh at myself.

A Good Italian Girl

"Hey, I was always a good Italian girl!" My girlfriend exclaimed at a recent dinner party while we were chatting over coffee after dinner. Our husbands were playing briscola - a card game - on the now cleared dinner table, fully distracted from any other activity surrounding them. Now that the dishes were done, we women could gather in our little circle and discuss our current unique family dramas and life stresses. Her comment struck me as funny as she was actually over 60 years old and no longer a girl but in fact, a Nonna of two grandchildren.

This phrase I can totally relate to and I have also used it in the past to refer to myself in some way or to justify why I did as I was expected to do, not necessarily what I really wanted to do.

This comment is not only about being a young girl; it actually means lots of different things in the ethnic female community. This phrase is what I refer to as the unwritten cultural expectations, rules and behaviours we have as ethnic women. The pre-defined box we are expected to fit into. This phrase means at times something that we have been told to do, or a tradition that we have automatically followed. This phrase means keeping the peace in the family and accepting the family dynamics for what they are and pushing our own desires or personal opinions aside for the good of the family or our parents. We remember that blood is, in fact, thicker than water and that family always comes first.

This phrase means that despite the adversity we face within our families and our own life pressures, we remain true to our family values and respect the connections we have together. Essentially, WE DO ALL THE 'RIGHT' THINGS IN LIFE FOR OUR FAMILY.

Ethnic women, me included, wear that description as a badge of honour. In fact, if I think about some of the dramas we have had to deal with, we certainly should all get a beautiful diamond encrusted badge for it and a fully catered ethnic ceremony where all the men and our children prepare and serve a meal to us ...

Hmmm…… I think that's what Mother's Day and birthdays are supposed to be about, right? Ok, stop the dreaming Claudia.

What happens when those who enforce the unwritten cultural expectations are no longer here?

For most of my life, I have felt that my journey as the child of an Italian immigrant raised in the western suburbs of Adelaide is what has made me so unique and resilient in this world. "They simply don't make them like us anymore," was my recurring thought.

However, last year, after 53 years of being a proud Giussa, and 'good' Italian girl, I started questioning who I really was at this stage of my life. Is this role, rules and the traditions that I maintain really relevant in this day and age?

Then in July 2020, my dad died suddenly from a heart attack in the midst of the global pandemic caused by COVID-19. The day after his passing, as we prepared for his funeral, I had an overwhelming feeling that all those rules I adhered to were now invalid and never really made a difference in this world. I felt reflective and wondered whether the struggle with my dad was really worth it in the end? What was its higher purpose? What is my purpose in this world and what will my legacy be to my children when I pass? Will I always feel this exhausted in life and have the feeling of cultural responsibility on my shoulders? Am I still on the right path in life? Why now, at this age, do I feel so lost in this world?

I feel those of us that were born in the 1960s and 70s are in many ways a lost generation. We are lost in the uniqueness of our situation and the fact that no other generation will ever experience the same environment we endured and therefore never really understand the meaning behind our mindset and our behaviours. I have this deep feeling of regret in the loss of time and life experiences during my childhood. Did the unwritten rules accomplish anything in the end? Was it about maintaining our traditional cultural uniqueness or was it all about controlling our behaviour according to our parents' needs?

I noticed through regular conversations with women my age and of similar ethnic backgrounds, that we are going through a similar journey. This journey is in stark comparison to the younger generation of ethnic women and very different to Anglo-Australian women. Anglo-Australian women can relate to us as women and mothers, yet despite living in the same country, many still cannot completely understand why we bother with all those traditions anymore. We are in fact a special breed of women who have endured adversity and who grew up required to comply because that was the way it was then, in that era, with our immigrant parents.

Unfortunately, I feel my generation of women have it twice as hard compared to our mothers due to our own high expectations of how perfect we think we must be, and how perfect everything around us must be. Perfect for everyone - except for ourselves.

Furthermore, I have started feeling anxious about how I instil those treasured family values in this technology-driven virtual society with my only child. I am challenged every day with my son's attitude and wonder if this is actually possible? Are the arguments with our own children about our values and expectations for them all worth it? Does it actually make any difference to them in the long run? How do I modernise our ethnic cultural values? Are our children considered ethnic as well? Do they feel ethnic like we did?

This book is about my personal journey, told through my proud Australian-Italian cultural eyes, and includes both the highs and lows of my life. I write about my experiences growing up within my family, the darkness I faced at times trying to understand the *why* and *who* of the person I became as a result of those ethnic experiences. It is also about my transformational journey: my awakening and taking the leap from feeling stuck to feeling inspired and re-energised. I have emerged as a different woman with new insight and inspirations to share with my fellow ethnic soul sisters and Giussas of the world.

This story and journey may be my own, however, I feel it is also a very similar one to my fellow ethnic soul sisters in Australia and maybe within some other areas of the world.

I used to believe that putting myself out there and being vulnerable with my feelings was being self-absorbed or weak. However, what I have learned through my previous writings about my IVF journey and my passion business, Shining Light, is how little I knew that others were struggling with the exact same thing I felt, and if I didn't show up, I might not ever have helped another individual in this world. So here I am … showing up from beneath my rock … full ethnic and Giussa style… stripped bare and vulnerable.

Part One

Where My Giussa Life Began

I was the third female child born at home in my parents' bedroom in the western suburbs of Adelaide in the middle of the night. I was born in a sudden onset of labour and delivered by my mother into a bedside table drawer. I came really quickly according to my mum who said she didn't have time to panic. However it could have been a dangerous situation for both of us.

My anxious dad called mum's friend Diana from across the road to help, while he rode his bike to our Italian aunty and uncle's house to use their phone to call the doctors. By the time he returned I was delivered safely, snuggled in a drawer filled with mum's good lingerie. (Well, I made that bit up! When I explain my delivery story I exaggerate and tell people that I came into the world in a hurry and was born into a drawer of luxury and that's why I have expensive taste and am always late and forever rushing around). The truth is that the silk nighties were in fact only cotton nighties, as my mother is a very practical Italian woman. Despite this, I always felt that my sudden urgency to be present in this world and be born at that time of day set the path for my determination in life to push myself forward when I need to show my true self and my own unique power. As I write this as an introduction to who I am, I don't think I have really analysed my birth delivery prior to this moment. The reality is that I was born in a drawer. A drawer is literally a box.

Oh my god! Was my feeling of being 'boxed in' and my resistance to being placed in a pre-judgemental box (figuratively speaking) all due to my birth story? I can't believe the symbolism of it all!

Growing Up and My Mother's Influence

My sisters and I grew up in an Italian environment with a slight variation because of my mother's Belgian upbringing and her belief that knowledge and study were the best way forward for herself and her four girls to achieve in life.

Italian women and mothers have the most impact on the family unit and our children. Our impact and attitude to life has more of an influential effect than what we possibly realise. When we are nurtured by resilient women, we then become resilient ourselves and empower our children to be the same. There is a flow-on effect that we must acknowledge and foster in a positive way.

Despite the private Catholic school education and extensive cultural activities that my mother carefully nurtured us through growing up, I felt I didn't really grow up as a true Australian-Italian, and my outlook on life often reflects this different start to the world. My sisters and I were not considered as having a full Italian upbringing as we also had a French/Belgian influence and this was often pointed out to us by our strict and sometimes opinionated Neapolitan aunty and later by my Neapolitan Italian mother-in-law.

When I finally married, my mother-in-law proudly announced to her friends that now that I was in their Italian family she was going to fine tune my Italian ethnic skills and teach me the "right" Italian traditional way. She didn't consider my mother to be a true Italian as she had a bit of French influence in her cooking and the way she did things. As I write this I am saddened and amazed by the subtle ethnic comments that have been said to me throughout my life regarding my upbringing and how I needed to better conform to the traditional ethnic women's roles, place and rules. My mother was born Italian, but she was just more of an educated and modern woman who conformed and played by my dad's Italians rules the best she could. So maybe I have always been on the outside or on the cusp of this Italian / Australian life that enveloped me (and also sucked the life out of me at times).

During my youth, my weekends with my sisters were filled with Saturday morning French language lessons at the Alliance Francaise d'Adelaide, Friday nights singing in an Italian Junior choir with the Italian Choral Art Society and Sunday morning Italian Mass in Croydon, a western suburb of Adelaide. On Sundays we occasionally performed around South Australia at the various Italian feasts with the Italian Junior Choir. Our mother also bought us tickets to see the ballet at the Festival Theatre on Sunday afternoons when the season started and took us on monthly visits to the city museum, art gallery, library and parks. We also regularly attended both Italian and French stage plays and films. Whilst cooking and cleaning, you would often hear French and Italian music being played by my mother. We were surrounded by French and Italian culture from a young age and throughout our teens.

We were not brought up to *only* cook and clean as our main purpose and skill in life. Although we still helped our mother every night in the kitchen, usually taking turns with the different tasks such as setting the table and dishes, and on Saturdays with chores and food shopping, our mother wanted us to feel that was not our only life's purpose as women in this world. Every Sunday after church we had our Sunday pasta with Braciola. The sauce had been simmering since the morning, tantalising us, and was ready to eat as soon as church was finished. That smell of sauce and braciola meat simmering on the stove served with pasta and crusty bread is something I will never forget nor stop yearning for the rest of my life. This simple traditional meal and sitting at the table together eating it is what I directly associate with my immediate family and beautiful childhood memories. It is my red string link to my heritage, my parents and my siblings. So simple yet so strong in evoking past memories.

Sundays was seen as our family day and we looked forward to having a regular Sunday afternoon outing to the city library, a park, Semaphore beach foreshore, or visiting family friends for afternoon coffee. My dad would go to the soccer with other men when the season was on during winter and mum would entertain us. There were no outings to fancy places to eat or paid events, and rarely would we actually be allowed any purchased treats, even an ice-cream. There simply was not a lot of extra money for the extras so mum often packed a little snack lunch from home with the Italian biscuits and coffee thermos. It was simply to get us girls out of the house for a bit to recharge and a nice walk out in the sunshine.

We also did all the regular things kids our age did, including riding our bikes, playing tennis on the road, playing board games, spinning our records and watching midday movies on the weekend: especially Elvis Presley, Jerry Lewis and Dean Martin.

There are a few traditional highlights during the year for most Italian families. These traditions are all linked to the land and harvesting food at a certain time of the month. I grew up eating produce from our back garden. This not only kept us fed all year round but it was dad's mindful escape on the weekends and his greatest pride. Each summer I recall helping him place the recycled wooden stakes in the ground for the planting of his 10 rows of tomato plants, and watching him dig the path of soil near each row where the water would soak into the ground for the plant's nutrients. I still remember the smell of ripening tomatoes from being sent to the garden to harvest the tomatoes for salad for lunch or dinner. I was taught to be careful going through the rows and pick only the ripe ones to eat and carefully leave the others on the stalk until they were ready. Being a bit of a tomboy, I was also allocated the task of helping my dad move the water sprinkler to each tomato row every night during summer to ensure the tomatoes were growing well and the dirt surrounding each row was well watered. This planting happened all his life along with the yearly fennel, spinach, lettuce and herbs together with our peach, mandarin and lemon trees. My dad was into organic produce and would not use chemicals. Everything was naturally grown and nurtured through the love of the land and the love from their Italian hearts and souls. Nothing can surpass home grown produce and many dinner recipes made throughout the year followed what was in our garden at the time.

Even to this day there is rarely a visit home to see my parents without departing with a bag of produce from the garden or lemons picked from the tree. This simple act is part of our heritage. We call them ethnic parcels of love.

Sauce day was one of the highlights of the year for my dad and all Italian families. He was the most excited this time of year. The lead up would be weeks in the planning. Firstly, mum and dad would drive to the tomato farmer and order the boxes of sauce tomatoes for a certain weekend and discuss the box purchase rate of tomatoes and what their other friends paid and who they were. During the year we spent time washing and storing the recycled beer bottles and glass containers. These items all had to be rewashed, sanitised, stacked and ready to go. The tomato boiling drum was retrieved from the shed and positioned for the items to be placed on the fire for boiling. A huge space under the carport was washed and cleared to place all the tomatoes on a blanket ready for washing and peeling, dicing and crushing. Everything around the sauce area was cleaned and every piece of equipment re-scrubbed and set up on tables for the production line of events. Everyone had their stations and their allocated jobs to perform. The day usually started at 5am and you kept going until it was all done and everything was completed and washed. The day was spent talking and laughing together while we worked, reminiscing and listening to Italian music. It was a circle of members all working and connected together. At night time my dad would anxiously ensure that the boiling bottles were safe and not breaking their seal before retiring for the night, exhausted but usually content. He would rejoice with the total number of bottles made that year. It was almost like winning the lotto: he would report to my mum the magic number of bottles made and what their reserve was in storage. Such a simple level of happiness but this one process connected them directly back to their home land, and their heritage. This sauce process and many other traditions like sausage and wine making kept them alive on the inside. For many Italians it is a thread that connects them to their own parents and childhood.

Outside attending our Catholic school and Sunday Italian mass, we were not allowed out with friends to simply just 'hang'. We didn't leave home to go anywhere without our parents' permission or without one of our sisters until we were 17 or 18 years old - and God forbid ever talk to a boy! These rules and scenarios were also standard amongst my school friends and generally most families were the same. Your cousins or very close family friends were seen as your only option for play dates. This usually occurred when the entire family would visit Saturday nights or Sunday afternoons and you were allowed to run wild around each other's houses and hang out together, away from the strict parents. This is very different to the current generation where we help our children to schedule play dates with children we don't even know very well or haven't even met the parents.

We had a very small family in Adelaide, with only a few cousins, so being with my sisters as constant play companions instilled a friendship and bond that still exists today. We often talk about the play things we did together in our backyard, especially all the pranks I personally would pull on all my sisters to create some excitement (my younger sister Celeste was easily pranked and usually ended up in tears). Ironically, these were the bedtime stories my son would request the most when he was little: silly stories of our backyard antics and making forts and structures from my dad's garage items. Marcus was especially proud of his mum's prank stories on his aunties and would brag to his cousins how his mum tricked their mums.

I never really thought to rebel too much as a child and young teen and accepted the strictness of the situation as it was. It was simply the Italian way of life and the family rules that you were expected to follow. I thought that 18 years old seemed to be the magic number for allowing me to make some of my own informed decisions; in a way I waited for that time in my life to pursue my own adventures in life and make decisions about my life moving forward.

As I write this, I remember questioning our parents' strictness, especially my dad's plans and what age he was anticipating us leaving our home and under what circumstances. At about 18 I had the courage to have the conversation with my father. I asked him how he was going to orchestrate his dream of all four of his daughters getting married when we were not allowed out of the house or allowed to go out with girlfriends to socialise? Did he think four boys were simply going to knock on our door and ask for our hand in marriage like in the old days? He would sadly be disappointed. I advised him that this was Australia not Italy and not the 1950s and none of his female children would ever support that concept. I suggested it was definitely time to change his thoughts and allow his daughters to go out so that we could meet our potential husbands (preferably unchaperoned by another sibling). I was always requested to take my sisters with me on my outings: little did he know that my sisters were not interested in hanging around watching me dance all night with my friends and talk to boys. My older sister in particular disliked the dance and club scene and would very occasionally give in to my pleading to take me out with my friends.

My mum would tell us the story about how she met my dad; she was introduced to him by one of her brothers who was living with him at the time in Belgium. She said that once he was introduced to her at 16 years old, he was smitten by not only her innocent sweet nature, but her mum's Neapolitan cooking and the big Italian family Sunday lunches that he was invited to each week. Dad had left his family in Italy to go to Belgium to make a living as a potter. He was all alone in a big city, working and sending part of his wages back to his parents each week to support them. The Sunday lunches with mum and her family was the start of their courtship. Mum jokingly told us that she didn't have a chance of meeting anyone else as my dad was determined to catch her! He was happy to wait until she turned 18 to marry her, despite there being an 8-year age gap. Mum said he was also in love with the family Italian pasta lunches and being part of an Italian family again. They did fall in love and did have the chance to spend some time alone outside the family with a chaperone. In those times that is how you met people: through a set up by your brothers or a family member and once in the door it was for keeps, especially if your family liked them as well. My dad would call my mum 'Chèrie': this means 'darling' in French. When they migrated to Australia my dad continued to call my mum this as her pet name and my Neapolitan aunty would often mimic them and call my mum 'Cherry'.

This was what my dad knew in terms of meeting your future life partner and courting. He was in no way prepared for his third Australian-born child Claudia born at home in a drawer to have her own thoughts on how she should meet her future life partner and live her own life by her own rules.

My parents changed slightly as time went on, however the watching and questioning remained constant for a while until I met my Australian-born, Italian boyfriend, John. I was the most vocal amongst my sisters about being allowed to go out and socialise. Normally the oldest paves the way in breaking some of the rules so that the younger siblings get a decent chance of living it up without so many restrictions, or - if you were lucky - a great brother that helped you meet some guys or drop you off to a club and then picked you up later or even let you hang with his friends way into the night without a curfew.

Nup, that wasn't my luck! My two oldest siblings were happy to go out occasionally, but not every weekend. They preferred to stay home on a Saturday night to watch a movie. We did not have any cousins my age to hang with and so I simply had to break the rules and cop all the flack and arguments that came with negotiating with my parents. This had a disastrous effect on our relationship, especially the power playing with my dad, as I simply didn't want to be placed in that box anymore and always told what to do.

In our home and I suspect in a lot of ethnic homes, money was the control mechanism used to deter my social behaviour. Without your own money you really couldn't go out. My parents were certainly not going to hand over their hard-earned money to allow their daughter go out when they were not happy with it in the first place!

As was the case with most ethnic children, we technically didn't get an allowance from our parents. We were simply provided with what we needed and on special occasions we got a few gifts and surprises along the way. The handing over of money or gifts was at the discretion of the parents and your behaviour always played a part in the level of generosity. As their children you were always provided for at home without any questions, no matter what age you were. There was certainly no expectation of paying board from my parents. But outings with your friends and drinking and dancing at clubs was another matter. In my parents' eyes this was not necessary in life.

In addition to being the loudest and the rule pusher I was also very resourceful and hard working. From the age of 16 I had always worked part-time. By the time I was 18, I was working regular hours at David Jones in the men's fragrances area. "Hey mum and dad, don't worry about me. I've got my own money to go out tonight." They couldn't hold me back now: I was full of solutions to their objections. The money I earned wasn't much per week, however it was enough to get into the dance clubs and have a few drinks at the venues. My mum always worked her kindness with me behind the scenes and filled my yellow Gemini car with petrol so her determined daughter at least had some wheels to get around! From about the age of 20, while juggling university and a part-time job, I was earning my own money, and I tried to break the rules when I could.

Well, let me define what I mean by breaking the rules. I was never a real "Rebel" or "Black Sheep". Those terms meant that you did what you want and you were causing trouble and not caring about others. I was never self-centred in my approach. I think I was - and still am - a people pleaser and don't like to hurt others' feelings. Breaking the ethnic rules does not actually mean what you would call breaking the rules in the real world of sex, drugs and rock and roll. It was for me simply being allowed to go out and leave the house when I wanted to socialise with my friends, nothing more than that. Essentially it was not asking permission to do things and deciding on my own accord under my own value system.

As I became more financial, I would go out dancing most weekends with my other Giussa ethnic girlfriends and mid-week we would go to see a band at a city pub. I fondly remember the Earl of Aberdeen in the city and the band Baked Potatoes. I had such a good time during that time of my single life with my girlfriends Vivian and Gina. I developed a love of Corona beers while we laughed and danced standing at the front of the band, singing at the top of our voices (and not necessarily knowing the words of the songs).

During this time of my regular weekly outings, my dad would remind me that if I ever came home pregnant, I would be asked to leave our home and have to fend for myself. "Ti raccomando" would be the phrase he would always use on me. ("I am warning you" is how best to say this in English).

He never made these comments to my other sisters, or when my sister Diana came out with me, as he assumed she would come to watch me and make sure I didn't get into any trouble.

Hey dad! Guess who used to get pissed easily? Umm, your other daughter not me! You should have told her "ti racommando" as well!

Being warned not to get pregnant every time I was getting ready to go out, I felt was somewhat offensive and a very passive aggressive Italian tactic. I understood that he wanted me to remain pure and a virginal Catholic walking down the aisle in white. Firstly, my parents were not even aware whether I was sexually active or not: it was simply said as a warning not to be, as pregnancy was the automatic result in their eyes. In fact, this part of the comment did not upset me as much, as I knew all parents of my generation and ethnic background had the same view. It was the regular comment of kicking me out of the house if it happened. Again, I felt that the safe haven your family and childhood home is supposed to provide was really only there if you played by the unwritten cultural rules. This comment would cause me recurring sadness during my 30's and 40's. It wasn't that I wanted to get pregnant young or out of wedlock. It was when I was struggling with infertility while I was married. I wished I had taken my chances and gotten pregnant earlier as that would have been a better outcome than the 20 years of sadness spent enduring infertility and IVF treatments.

Hindsight or did I just get jinxed Italian style?

My sisters and I also had a code of silence thing going on with our parents: we never wanted any of us to get into real trouble so we would never tell on each other and would often simply pretend not to know anything. Most of our friends were the same, especially if we got quizzed by each other's parents.

The hiding of information and fearfulness of our parents was a universal thing in our ethnic circle of friends. I know other male friends who had been in car accidents or really, really drunk and relying on friends to collect them from the scene or rescue them, instead of calling their parents. We all knew the amount of grief they would have received from their parents would have been more than they could handle, especially the ongoing feeling of disappointment.

Reflecting back and now as a parent I feel that this situation of running out the door to meet my friends with my parents having very little information of where I was going is not what I would want for my own child. I want to be fully aware of where they are going and that they are safe. I remember being in some not so safe situations and walking down some dangerous Adelaide city streets on my own to get to my car to drive home: at times with too much alcohol in my system. Please note: I am not implying that I was not a good Italian girl walking the streets, my curfew was actually 1am (so not very late anyway) and I was usually in groups of other ethnic girls. The simple fact was that we had such a hard time being allowed to enjoy ourselves, even on a normal level with friends drinking and dancing and simply having fun, that we never disclosed what we were doing for fear of reprimand and privileges being removed and the ultimate judgement. We were scared of our parents and we didn't want their disapproval and then the guilt that came with that, so we ensured they never found out. You may find it odd that I talk about removal of privileges even though I was 20 years old and an adult. In our ethnic circles you were never an adult until you left home to get married, and you were technically never kicked out of home so that you could fend for yourself. It was the guilt and grief they gave you while you were at home if you didn't follow the rules which made you feel ashamed. You would hear it constantly retrospectively and the comments would go on forever. They would tell the other relatives: "Did you hear what my child did? Oh, where is the respect … blah, blah."

Another discussion I would regularly have with my father was the concept of having the opportunity and encouragement to undertake further education. I knew this was actually my mother's encouragement. "Why are you even bothering encouraging and supporting us to be further educated if our opinion is then not allowed to be taken into consideration? Is your opinion the only one that counts? And when you say "No" then that is the end of the discussion. What is the whole point? Do we even bother asking anymore?"

"While under my roof it is my way," was his standard answer.

My father would have been happy once we finished high school and started working. Then we could start saving our money ready for a deposit on a house and our wedding once we met our future husbands. You're reading this and perhaps thinking: what about a holiday? Well, we could do that. But only if we went to Italy to see the relatives and stayed at their houses under their careful watch. But not an adventure holiday to some exotic destination, or God forbid a gap year after year 12 exams (which is what Claudia wanted to do). Or maybe work overseas or one of those American working holiday adventure camps things helping kids. "Why would you want to do that?" Or "too dangerous…not safe for you." "We can't keep an eye on you", would be just some of my father's responses. "It is better that you go to university and get a good education and a great earning job for the rest of your life," would be my mother's recommendation. Go with the flow, don't rock the boat, play by the rules, was the underlying message.

We four girls absorbed the strictness and learned to navigate the rules and go on and do what we had to do in our lives. However, looking back, it was also hard for my mother. She was trying to fit into a culture that was foreign to her despite her strict Italian poor upbringing in Belgium. In addition to that she also left her closest family - including five sisters - behind and did not have the same family closeness in Australia like she had with her sisters. It was my resilient mother that convinced my father to move to Australia for a better life for themselves and their children. My mother was the one that organised all the sponsorship paperwork with the Belgian government and co-ordinated the move to my uncle's house in Adelaide. My parents arrived on a Qantas plane with four suitcases and two children on their laps in 1966.

I was born a year later and during my time at home with her, she did correspondence lessons and learned to read and write English so that she could then go to work and help her husband support the family. She was the mum, the wife, the homemaker and now full-time worker.

Despite this full work load she taught us that you simply get on with it, work hard, keep looking forward and do the best for your family with the skills you have. I watched her struggle with the balance of full-time work and the home. I saw her regularly exhausted but resilient. She rarely put her needs and passions first. She was always serving her husband and her family and did what was expected of her. This perseverance at all costs and work hard attitude never wavered, even though her life was tough with my dad controlling the family decisions. Her four girls also followed her lead and worked too hard and her exhaustion would then match her girls' exhaustion by the time they all reached 50. They also thought they could try to achieve it all, sacrificing many of their own dreams for a life that was not necessarily their chosen vision of how life would turn out and far from the opportunities and adventures they dreamed of.

My mother would later tell me that she worked hard at trying to protect us girls from the Italian environment by encouraging education and cultural activities. She hoped this would divert our attention away from the typical Italian community opinions and our father's strictness and the negativity and discrimination towards a girl's role in life. My dad was concerned with what people would say and think if we ever did something that went against the cultural rules. He would remind us that - as girls - we were only allowed to do certain things, and this strictness was for our own good. My mum had been on the receiving end of this treatment in Belgium as an Italian immigrant and was facing it also in Australia as an adult female immigrant. Her strategy was to keep us busy and focus on things outside of the home to bring joy in our lives. She taught us cooking and cleaning skills but did not focus on these tasks as being our only skills in life or that they would bring us great joy. Her aim was that - despite knowing we would be affected by the cultural standards that automatically surrounded us - by raising us to be strong, open minded and ambitious women it would help us in the long run, no matter where life might lead us. I always felt that at least my mum understood my determination and drive to experience life and push the confines of the pre-determined box. She knew I was different from her other daughters and she would often remark how much I was like her entrepreneurial, fun loving, kind-hearted and cheeky younger brother, Joseph. Despite not knowing him, I felt that his determination and successful business life was something I could also achieve. Knowing that I get this internal drive from some family member on the other side of the world made me feel better.

It seemed that in the 1980's and 90's our cultural community, including my father, felt that further education, careers or personal hobbies were only useful until we met our husbands. Or if by some chance we were still unmarried, then we would be able to support ourselves and earn a decent income to save for our own house and life. This was our perceived value as females, along with the focus on cooking and cleaning. The ability to focus on our own needs or interests until we met our future husbands was seen as a good use of our time until the day our real role in life started. I always felt this influence and obligation growing up and so did my girlfriends. This destiny might have been totally okay with some females in my generation however I always felt that my dream of having my own career to nurture and fulfil me would not stop me from being a great wife or mother. I never felt that there was a one or the other option, or that we ethnic women are any less of a wife with whatever we personally choose in life as our own preference.

The ethnic rule book made it clear that my value was as a wife and mother, supporting the family in the home, cooking and cleaning. This didn't mean that I was not expected to earn money and contribute to the family income. It was that I wasn't expected to aspire to higher levels in my work or career, or pursue further education. My value was as a good Italian girl that followed the unwritten ethnic rules.

This reminds me of how our perceived future was determined at such a young age as ethnic females, even within our extended family and friends. In the 80's I remember having my First Communion with my sister Diana when we were about 10 years old. We had a joint celebration at home with all of our family and friends. We were opening our gifts and I received a pink jewellery box with a wind-up dancing ballerina from my godmother, Luisa. I remember thinking how wonderful and special my gift was. This was probably the only real kids present we received that day. Our other gifts were mainly towels and fine linen ('biancheria') from some of the older relatives. I remember asking my mum what I was going to do with all these other presents? She announced that she would put them in my Biancheria (Glory Box) and save them for my own home when I got married. I was 10 at the time! Imagine giving a 10-year-old girl in this era for her communion celebration a box set of towels and linen for her married home.

Please, people! What were they even thinking back then?!

You know the funny thing was, when I did move into my own home at the age of 29, I received all these items back to me in a box from my mum. She had kept all the towels, tablecloths and beautifully embroidered Italian linen that we received from our ethnic relatives throughout our childhood. I saw those bright yellow towels with the brown flower embroidery in the original 80's brown box packaging and my name on them. My Communion Day flashed before me and I thought: "Oh my God, the towels! I get to use them now after 19 years in storage. I'm in my own home and married and my dowry gifts have followed me." The symbolism hit me then and I laughed at how long it had taken to finally officially be able to rip the box open to use the yellow towels. The downside was that they were the old, smaller style and so they barely fit around my now larger body (and they were pretty ugly). I remember my husband asking me what was with the "ugly yellow towels" hanging in the bathroom and if I had actually purchased them myself to complement our blue and white bathroom. My answer was: "Oh no honey, I got them for my communion and I'm using them as I qualify to open that box now that I am married."

Ironically I still have all the linen and "glory box" items given to me in my home linen cupboard. They have remained there for 24 years with the occasional restack and reflection. Due to space restriction in our home my husband often remarks that I should just ditch everything in that cupboard I do not use. John would comment: "Be realistic Claudia. All the old stuff especially, you're never going to use it." My reluctance to part with it is something that he would not understand being brought up as an ethnic boy. It represents a link to my younger self like a red string that connects me to my past journey. It shows me how far I have come to be my own person and how much things have changed from generation to generation.

I feel that no one knows what life scenarios I will be presented with in the future. I might pass them on to my future daughter-in-law or female family member and talk about my journey. Or alternatively I might repurpose them into tie dye linen items or make vintage tote bags with the beautiful Italian material and sell them on EBAY and start a new fashion trend.

Omg, there you go again Claudia! Those business ideas keep popping out of your head, girl! You were born an entrepreneur I am certain of it.

Because we were born female, we were expected to be pretty little things and play quietly and be polite. As girls we were complimented on how beautiful and well-mannered we were by other family members and the community. That was the standard of achievement that we were encouraged to aspire to (and even better if we loved to cook from an early age). My family certainly reprimanded me for being boisterous, especially compared to my other sisters. I was always reminded that I wasn't as girly or as studious and serious as my sisters, especially my older two sisters. Strangely, my mother had this thing about dressing my sister Diana and myself in the same outfit like twins, even though we were one year apart. Now, Diana was girly and I was not. She was thin with beautiful olive skin, long black hair, big brown eyes and was quietly spoken. I had blonde hair, fair freckled skin, curvier, long legs, and was loud! I wanted to run, climb and ride bikes and be outside, whereas she was more of an indoor girl. Yet my mum always dressed Diana and myself the same: same dress, shoes and hair. I was just in the next size up. I now look back on photos and see my dress ruffled and socks down and my big cheesy smile in the photo, while Diana looked the picture perfect 'good Italian girl'. My sisters and I accepted ourselves for who we were and we did not compete with each other in that way. It was always others that pointed out our differences. Maybe I was born to break the rules and be my own version of a good Italian girl. Despite always being reminded to be less loud and more girly (and really, let's face it, more proper and subservient), I ignored their comments and reminded myself that our family needed my personality and so did the rest of the world. Furthermore, I was actually born a Scorpio on that fateful night and we have our own unique set of next level character traits! Living by our own rules is one of our traits.

Based on this perception, when I was growing up, I always wished I was a born a boy. This was not because I actually wanted to be a boy as I love being female. However being born a boy represented more freedom and also the encouragement by our culture to aspire and learn. It was expected that boys would be the bread winner of the family and that only boys' educational development would count in the long term: they were encouraged to dream big and aspire at business.

My father was often given condolences that he never had a son and only daughters. They would say: "Poor Carmine … all girls." I did feel that I really missed out on not having a brother's influence in my life. Although, the flip side is that there would have been a clear and direct inequality within our own family between what girls and boys were expected to do and achieve. We four girls and mum knew that my dad would have treated our potential brother differently.

I felt the inequality indirectly and observed it from afar in other families. Once I met my husband I also saw it in his family unit. I believe that having a brother would have changed my upbringing in many different ways. We would not only be serving our father at the dinner table but also our brother. This is sometimes a hard thing for brothers and sisters to deal with as siblings. However, I believe it depended on whether their parents treated them within the family unit as equals, or differently because they were male. Ultimately, our message as Australian-Italian females was that we were there to serve our men, including our dad, brother and husband.

The Giussa Road Block and Turning Point

During my teens I felt aspiring to big dreams was a waste of my energy. My role would be to simply support my husband and serve my family. I struggled with this growing up as a young teen. I lost motivation to achieve at school, despite knowing it was a financial struggle for my mum to send us to a private girls' school. My father would complain that it was a waste of financial resources as I was not achieving academically and that I obviously didn't care.

I felt there was no point in some ways, so I spent a lot of time being a clown in the classroom and making my friends laugh. I felt that my life would magically make sense and fall into place once I left school, started working and married the man of my dreams and had my own family. I felt at that time anything else I did was just a time diversion. My path was looking like this despite my own vivid imagination and dreams of travelling the world and leaving Australia to explore outside my box.

After years of accepting this perceived role in my Australian-Italian life and just moving through life and school, I hit a major road block at the end of year 11. We had just returned from a family trip to Italy, France and Belgium. I always thought that I would go to university despite my school clown antics. I was aspiring to study management and work in a creative advertising role as I had successfully completed work experience in this area and loved the creative side of it as well as the strategic management side.

My school career counsellor informed me that I had not scored well in my assignments during the year, participated poorly and that as I didn't complete all my final exams due to my family's overseas holiday (probably not the best option in hindsight), as a result I only managed to achieve C and D grades for my subjects. This meant I therefore had not achieved a place in year 12 Matric as I had not reached their expected grade point average. She advised that I would certainly fail year 12 based on my marks, which would have an effect on my personal esteem. Despite asking for the opportunity to complete year 12 and then repeat it if necessary, I was simply not allowed. I discovered the reason for this later: the school was protecting its school ranking year 12 average. The career counsellor continued to advise that my only option was to move into the secretarial class for my final year if I wanted to stay at this particular school. She warned that I probably would not have the skills to achieve a university qualification such as management based on my current marks. She suggested TAFE as my best option, and advised me to consider an easier qualification to achieve based on my abilities.

I remember staring at her after she spoke to me and my mum at that school meeting and thinking, "Hey lady if you think I am going to allow you to tell me what I can or cannot achieve in life - watch this space."

I remember feeling deflated and angry at the same time. I was upset and felt that there was already enough direct discrimination around me in my current life from my cultural community. I was being bombarded by the message that there were limits to what I could achieve, simply because I was born a girl. The only expectation was that I finish school, get a job, get married, have babies and serve my family for the rest of my life. This was my destined path and expected journey.

In my head all I heard was, "Yes Claudia, you can support your husband and family. That is your best role in life and what you were born to do. After all you are just a good Australian-Italian girl... an 80's Giussa... that is all you are. There is no need for you to really aspire to do anything big or have your own dreams! You can support other people's dreams and learn to serve them well."

My life outlook and plan changed the moment I walked out of that career counsellor's office.

Yes, I might be a loud, giggly, talkative, shoulder pad and mini-skirt wearing, long-legged 80's Giussa girl with high hair. But don't you dare put me in a box and tell me that I cannot achieve my own personal dreams and aspirations in life because of my gender and nationality, and that my success in life will be only from serving and supporting other people!

Who are you in my life to tell me my future? Who are you to put me in that pre-judgemental box?

Va funculo lady!!

You now watch this ethnic Giussa chick go for it. I will show you my strength, bravery and my stubborn Italian chick Giussa power. Game on! You will not see me crumble despite this fall!

So what happened next was both fearful and courageous at the same time. I had decided I was not going to take the easy option and go to another school, despite getting into another seniors college for year 12. I was still devastated and felt like a school failure and loser. I lost most of my friends in my original class as I felt excluded from their activities by the school and I then subsequently avoided them in the school yard for the remainder of their graduating year. I was so hurt by it all... *But I had a plan.*

I decided that my best chance was to repeat my year 11 classes at the same school and get high enough scores to enter into year 12, then succeed at year 12 exams and get into the university course that I wanted to do. I became a nerd and studied every chance I had. I scored highly in my repeated year 11 class and the following year 12 year.

My parents were stunned with my transformation and dedication, and supported me every step of the way. Anything my family could do to help me during this journey was provided. This included endless cups of percolated coffee which I became addicted to during exam study times. The change was dramatic during those years and I became very serious and determined to prove my worth. Those red flags were now raised and I was not going to fail myself again.

The end result was that I did achieve the desired outcome and entered university on the first round of placements. I achieved a 90 matric scoring and a Geology school award and prize for scoring a Distinction in Geology and class effort. This failed year 11 student ended up walking on the school stage in her final year to personally accept an award from the school principal, who told me how proud she was of my hard work and achievements.

Yep, thanks Mrs Career Counsellor! What did you say? I was not good enough to get into university and could only be a secretary? Well, I now have a degree in management from University of South Australia as well as 3 other separate qualifications. Most importantly, unlike you, I have empowered many people through delivery of my training programs, career counselling and workplace coaching. I am also an entrepreneur and have two small business ventures that I have started and successfully run.

On the flip side a few good things also happened to me during that difficult journey at school.

By the time I finished high school I realised that failure didn't define me. Failure at school is something that happened. It's not who I am or who I will be. I had to learn to move on and be open to new opportunities and the possibility that I will fail again. Failure is an opportunity to learn, grow and evolve. However, it's often hard to remember that when things are not going your way. Shaking off that shame of failure was not an easy task at that age. However, in hindsight, I am glad that I learnt to pick myself up and move forward and that I learnt that lesson early in life.

Secondly, in my repeat class I found my new best friend - and fellow Giussa - Vivian. We have laughed and cried together at the happy and sad events in our lives ever since school, and we have supported each other to the core. I am a better person in this world because of her and we are better ethnic females and Giussas facing the world together. She is not only my Giussa soul sister for life but part of my forever family.

This stumble in the journey of life was also the start of a fire within me. It played a significant role in the way I would handle some aspects of my life, friendships and employment moving forward. It was not only that I had finally got my act together and started using my intelligence to achieve academically. This event changed what I was willing to accept in my studies and future employment. I now believed that learning new skills and working hard to try new things could lead to new opportunities and my happiness in life. There would no longer be a box confining me, stopping me in my career path. There would no longer be people telling me in my academic and professional life that I was not good enough.

I focused on being both brave and courageous and actively made myself learn new things, work outside my comfort zone and try adventurous activities in an attempt to extend my world outside my cultural expectations and the environment surrounding me.

I dreamed of a career and life that is aligned to my values or passion. One where I would find joy in the work I do on a daily basis and be part of something that I am good at and that energizes me.

My desire is to be truly at home with myself and live my own dream life and I truly believe I can have it the way I have envisioned it. A life free of guilt and obligations. A life that is equal and fulfilling on all levels.

Most of all I aspire to be truly at peace with the past and be present in the moments in front of my eyes.

Meeting Other Giussa Ethnic Chicks at University

After my huge high school effort to achieve a place at university, I felt quite anxious starting my uni degree. The course was three years long and I was to be in management the moment I graduated (well that's what I thought in my head naturally - since I was actually doing a management degree!) However as all we Giussas have learned, the workplace reality is quite different: they often didn't care what that piece of paper said and I had to prove myself all over again.

For the first few months I spent a lot of time in the library studying. But I'll never forget the day a vibrant beautiful blonde named Gabi walked confidently into class; she looked like she knew what she was doing in this world. I could tell she was a fellow ethnic chick with attitude and a unique fashion style. The school bag she carried around with her was a pink briefcase and she drove a hotted up yellow VW which I thought was a bit odd initially, but it suited her confidence. I would later discover it was all bravado and she was a fellow Giussa that was just trying to wing her confidence and succeed in this world just like myself. We both had huge dreams and we both came from working class families in the western suburbs of Adelaide. Gabi had an Australian-Polish background and was the eldest daughter of Polish immigrant parents. A short time later we would meet two other Giussas in our lectures, Effie and Kath, who were both the daughters of Greek immigrant parents. The first two years we were like the awesome foursome hanging out together at university and having fun. In my final year I changed to a part-time status and met another awesome ethnic Greek chick with huge hair, on trend fashion style and confidence named Dina. Together we all studied hard and supported each other to get over the last hurdle and graduate.

We became a team of ethnic girls determined to help each other and succeed together, but also have fun while doing it. We would save seats for each other, share study notes and help each other with assignments and research. Outside this study we were also determined to laugh and have fun and enjoy our uni life. We would have coffees and go on shopping trips in the city instead of going to uni lectures, play cards in the cafeteria with the other ethnic boys who were doing the construction course, go to uni parties together, party and dance at Adelaide clubs, talk all things boys and our future plans and dreams in life. We were surrounded by other friends in our class and we connected with many others in our business study stream. However we ethnic Giussas always looked out for each other and supported each other. What a combination and what a fun ride we had together, laughing, crying and stressing over assignments and exams. We all pulled each other up when we were down and not coping with the pressure of university, life and boys. We helped each other to succeed and to feel confident in life. This was the Giussa chick girl connection and once it was made it was usually made for life, no matter where your life took you: that sort of connection came from deep within the soul. Giussa chicks are connected via our cultural mind, spirit and soul.

Our finance lecturer remarked to us in our final year that we might have to find an organisation that would give us all a job together once we graduated. We were judged for lack of focus at times because of our close friendship and giggly nature. We were written off as simply ethnic girls studying that will not lead to anything great or successful in life, except maybe family planning. Luckily, we were brought up to be good polite ethnic females and taught not to answer back and respect teachers and authority. If they insulted anyone else they would have received a mouthful. Instead we just smiled and said to ourselves: "Watch us. We will let you know."

It was a huge effort getting to the end but we all did it: all the Giussas graduated with a Bachelor of Business (majoring in Marketing) from the University of SA. We all ended up in successful business management roles, separately though, not working together as predicted. Gabi travelled the world for her work as a fashion buyer and three of us, myself included, commenced our careers in the financial sector. We all got married, had children, juggled motherhood, life and worked successfully in the corporate world and became happy, well-adjusted intelligent individuals.

So, take that Mr Finance Lecturer! We were listening to your boring lectures but it's a shame you judged us on the surface level only. Yes, we are ethnic women but we also had dreams of a career and using our intelligence as well as looking after our families. Never underestimate our commitment.

Oh hey, Mrs Career Counsellor: I got a degree from university.

This time together was monumental for all of us and these women all still have a huge positive impact on my life today. We found each other at the age of 18 and we are still close friends despite the geographical distance between us. I relish the connections that I made all those years ago with my fellow ethnic Giussas, Gabi, Effie, Kath and Dina. One Polish, three Greeks and an Italian. Sounds like a comedy act routine in the making! In fact, we are soul sisters united forever.

It was simply assumed by some that we would not achieve anything big with our degrees. I'm not sure why there was this judgement from others. Yes, we were ethnic females that would probably marry and have families and maybe take a career break to care for them, but why would that disadvantage us or discourage us from completing our course or forging a successful career? We were all smart and driven and we believed that we could achieve anything we put our minds to. Maybe that drive came from the migrant cultural background that we all grew up in. It was a drive within all of us and one that we didn't need to explain to each other. We all knew that hard work and determination was going to secure our success in the world, just like our parents had taught us. Our parents also expected us to work hard at our studies and achieve this outcome. If we were going to waste our time we would have been told by our parents to stop wasting time and get a job instead. We were first-generation immigrant children and we understood that – this is a classic unwritten rule scenario. We knew we were given opportunities to study and be supported while living at home, so we were also expected by our families to follow through, achieve our goals and finish what we started. We were not at university to play and muck about; the expectation was there underneath at all times. I'm not sure where that perception from the lecturers came from, maybe it was that simple giggly Giussa nature. All I can say is never underestimate my ability to work hard and achieve my outcome. My high school experience showed me that through failure you can learn who you really are as an individual. The real failure is in fact never trying in the first place or not picking yourself up and trying again. Our work ethic came from our parents: we watched them work hard to provide for us and we were also expected to do the same. We were expected to work hard the rest of our lives and not squander any opportunity given to us. This was the reason they immigrated in the first place. To give us opportunities. They sacrificed their families and birth country to do that for us - their kids. We felt that responsibility and we carried that weight of their decisions on our shoulders. We not only had to achieve our dreams but also validate that their decisions and sacrifices were worth all the heartache.

Going Out Giussa Style

Just as we were called Giussas, boys from ethnic backgrounds were referred to as Marios. We were basically innocent girls and boys hanging out together with our friends and enjoying each other's company. Many of us were just like mates, while others became someone's boyfriend and girlfriend, whether that was short term or long term. All of us were simply all together, single or coupled, having a good time dancing and drinking together. We were enjoying our youth with an understanding of each other's cultural background, rules and home life. We were not out on the prowl for a one-night stand or just to be picked up. (Although that did happen for some Giussas, let's not sugar coat it and definitely no judgement). Generally, these boys knew our type and either connected with us on some level or went to sow their wild oats elsewhere, where the rules of engagement were not so strict and not for the rest of their lives.

We all would usually go out in groups of females or with sisters and brothers and cousins and friends of friends. The parents preferred it this way as they saw it as a safe option and that we would all look out for each other. Someone was the designated driver for the night and safely dropped everyone home at the end of the night, negotiating the drop off route according to each person's curfew. We would often speed from suburb to suburb to achieve each other's curfew so that our friends wouldn't get into trouble by their parents. We knew that most of our parents waited up and didn't sleep until we were home in bed. The breaking of the curfew and the resulting consequences was not something you wanted to happen to your friend. The next day they certainly would pay for it through the early morning penalty rises or extra allocated house work tasks given to them, along with a dash of disappointed looks and guilt over the lunch table. In my case it was the no excuses allowed for missing Italian mass no matter how tired I was, and lunch time dishwashing duties before I could sneak in a nap.

The fact that we were going out on the town and socialising was our version of breaking or bending our parents' rules. A far cry from what many others did and still a very innocent outing, yet it was new for us. It didn't stop us from being given the third degree whenever we announced we were going out. We would always get the twenty questions: "Out? Where? With who? Why? Who'll drop you home? When will you come home? Every day out, out. Is this a house or a hotel?!"

How different times are now. We request our kids text us no matter what time of the day or night to let us know of any delays in returning home, or expect the text asking to stay out longer or the pick-up location has changed. We are so much more accommodating and respectful of their personal time with their friends. That stress we experienced trying to get home not to miss our curfew and disappoint our parents is something I have not seen as being instrumental to implement with my own child. All I request is communication of the real scenario and the awareness of keeping himself safe.

As Giussas despite our bravado, we were not usually the most confident females. Our parents didn't raise us to be confident and forthright. They raised us to be nice and polite and respect people and wait to be asked or spoken to and not too loud. I'm not sure whether that was a good thing or not (and some Giussas had different variations of being loud and I was really not that loud in comparison).

There were some iconic clubs that really defined the 80's and 90's in Adelaide. On Saturday nights for our group of friends it was Rio's, Jules, the Old Lion, or St Pauls. Then on Sunday nights it was the Italian Club in Carrington Street, followed by coffee at Alfresco's on Rundle Street. The Italian club was a Sunday night club dedicated to ethnic girls and boys. It was totally fine that you were dropped off by your parents out the front as everyone else's parents did that. Then the club closed at 11pm so the pickup was again by a dad or older sibling, who had been given strict instructions not to loiter too close to the entrance, or preferably, to pick up further down the street.

We drank, listened to bands and danced on this huge dance floor and met other ethnic girls and boys. It was lots of innocent fun and one of those types of places where you always ran into someone you knew. We would connect with our friends, laugh, dance, drink and most importantly, meet boys.

I was quite shy around boys, as were some of my friends. We felt confident hanging out in a group. This gave us the confidence to walk into a party or club together and then stand around in a protective circle and check out the boys. We would hope that the boys would have the courage to come over and talk to us or at least make some mutual eye contact.

There was always some couple pashing in the dark corner or escaping to the car park for a bit of action. That was also part of the attraction of it all in some ways; it was happening around you like a normal club but definitely less sleazy and not something you felt that you had to participate in if you didn't want to. Everyone simply connected in groups of friends, you met a boys' group, they met your girls' group and everyone mingled together. A few might get together or at the very least, you have made friends with another ethnic individual in the world of Adelaide. We weren't there to technically meet the man who would be our future husband, but that's how it happened for some people. That was our version of connecting with people, not through phones or texting, just swapping numbers after the night or simply meeting up at the same place the following week.

I always remember the last song of the night was usually a slow one and then "bang" all the lights would turn on and the entire place would be illuminated. Just like when you parents would come into your room in the morning and switch the light on to wake you up for school. Same thing at this club: lights on, come on kids that's your cue now to go home and wait outside to get picked up by your parents. Such a simple time of life.

We were very innocent in our approach and not very forthright. Many of us just wanted to be able to enjoy ourselves and meet other like-minded people that we were attracted to. We wanted to feel like we were living in this bigger world outside our families.

My friends and I met lots of Marios during our early twenties. Some of the Marios I met were not the type of boys that I would go out with, but I made some great male friends and we had some great times together, laughing and joking around. Amazingly I am still friends with some of them all these years later, along with their wives and kids. Some great bonds of friendship were formed during these formative years of my life.

It was very easy going and innocent times and I feel those days are not the same for our children. The environment to meet other people has now changed. It is very technology driven and some are very self-absorbed and image conscious, forever ready to outshine each other and grab their five minutes of fame. The Italian Club is definitely not something our kids would want to be part of today. Just like we didn't want to be part of the set-up arrangements our parents were subjected to. Each generation evolves, yet somehow I feel saddened by our children's reliance on technology to communicate and connect. We were definitely part of some very unique times that were never to be repeated. There is nothing better than human face-to-face contact to really connect at a deeper and authentic level. The universal truth is that we are all connected to one another.

Meeting Your Future Partner: An Australian-Italian Boy

Another life changing event was meeting my husband and being part of another Neapolitan Italian family. I was in my final year of university when we met through friends at a drag racing event in Adelaide's North. God knows why I was even at such an event as it certainly was not my style to be hanging around car enthusiasts or car racing dragsters. My parents would have been horrified if they knew I attended: which they didn't. I was being a good friend and accompanied my girlfriend to this event. She had planned to meet up with a boy who turned out to be a friend of John's. From the moment I met John, he made me laugh and he had such an easy-going nature that was different from anyone I had met. He was the ultimate street-car loving ethnic boy with tight jeans, a mullet and adidas sneakers. Not my style of boy at all! I thought the attraction to him would be short lived. My now husband John of nearly 25 years is an ethnic boy with ethnic family values, a kind caring heart, loving dad and the friendliest person you would ever meet. He is the type to welcome everyone into his home and is the first to stop to help anyone in need.

So many good times were had during this phase of my life and so many great family moments with extended family and the

Molinara community. The diversity of individuals I met throughout my life who are connected to me through my husband John has been huge, and has expanded my circle of friendship far and wide as a result. Meeting John was definitely a life changing event and consequently my ethnic radar was going to be on overdrive for the rest of my life. My life changed at this point and I would never have the same ethnic life experiences as my sisters moving forward from that moment on. I was born into the same ethnic family with the same parents, but my life rules and cultural expectations just increased by 100%. All because I was going out with an ethnic boy. My dad was super proud that I ended up with someone he wished for all his girls, and that I would have to follow the rules he always expected me to. I always thought this trophy would have naturally gone to one of my calmer, more compliant sisters, not myself. I would learn some of the biggest lessons in life about human nature for the next twenty years whilst trying to meet those cultural rules and obligations.

The ethnic courtship rules were really difficult to conquer and again I was surrounded by new sets of rules with no actual instructions. After finally introducing my boyfriend John to my parents, I noted that my dad was definitely pleased and seemed to relax a little: he even extended my curfew to 1.30am! Woo hoo! Apparently he felt that with John I was a bit safer and more protected from the big world at night. I didn't really see his point to be honest and the amount of "pashing" we did in his car when we said goodnight parked all the way down the street would have definitely not impressed my dad if he knew.

I had been going out with John for about 12 months when my dad decided to have a little chat with me about the rest of my life. I knew something was brewing in his mind as my dad never had polite and quiet reflective chats with me. That was usually reserved for my older sister, Laura. I was used to arguing with him and feeling he disapproved of my behaviour. That's simply how we rolled. But that night my dad started telling me in Italian how pleased he was with how I had turned out and that I finished my studies and found a good job at a bank. He was also pleased that I was with John: a good Italian boy from a good family. He continued to say that I needed to start thinking about planning my wedding and getting married. This would naturally be the next step for me now in my life. I remember the conversation so clearly and the feeling of my heart dropping with sadness and fear and thinking *OMG they really expect me to marry now. I haven't managed to breathe and live a little or travel anywhere and he is expecting me to actually get married. What the hell? Was this the plan for me the minute I met someone and brought them home? Is he for real?* I screamed "MUUUUUUUM come here please."

Surely after a year of dating my first serious boyfriend you do not expect me to get married, do you? I advised my parents that I was thinking that I could finally start living my own life and make my own decisions and there was no way in hell I would get married just because they told me to. I advised them that the discussion was closed and not to bring it up again unless I brought it up. I had finally found my voice in my own home at the age of 23 years old. Needless to say, my dad was most unimpressed! My courtship with

John was actually a very long 8 years before John officially proposed and we started planning our wedding.

Did I just get jinxed again there? I really wasn't anticipating an 8 year wait when I made all those statements to my parents!

During this time I still felt the pressure from my parents to settle down a bit, especially by my dad. Although he did a huge turnaround once we introduced both parents to each other a few years after dating. In his mind I was settled and committed to a good Italian boy and he could relax a bit now that his determined stubborn daughter would be travelling the right path as John was by my side now.

At this time, I felt like things were shifting and changing. The ethnic way of life and bubble my parents contained me within while I was growing up had expanded for a short time. For a while I had felt that I was released in a hot air balloon floating free, being able to see the world from a different perspective and now I was back on the way down being pulled back by the sandbags and ropes to be repositioned back on land on a new path. The new role as a girlfriend and future wife to John and the new cultural rules that came with this new position was about to redefine my life. Things were about to change now. I could feel that I was moving from one set of rules and expectations to another. Same, same but different.

The Ethnic Courtship Travel Rules

Now that I was part of a couple, the ethnic rules were more stringent about where we could go together compared to being single and going away with my girlfriends. I had not travelled much during my life as my parents were not confident travellers and only started travelling once they had retired. As a family we only completed one overseas trip to both Italy and Belgium to see where our parents grew up and meet all our extended family. Once I started working, I could afford to travel. I have always had a burning desire to see the world and experience other cultures. At the age of 22 I was scheduled to go away with my girlfriends for 3 weeks on an overseas holiday to Greece and then to see my family in Belgium. This was about 3 months after I met John. My mum insisted I take my sister Diana with me as she had not travelled much either. My sister, the forever chaperone. We went and we all had a great time together as five ethnic Giussa girls navigating overseas travel. Upon my return I definitely had the travel bug and wanted to experience more travel destinations, especially with my boyfriend John.

However, much to my disappointment, I was not allowed to go with my boyfriend anywhere that was overnight or away unless we were married. This was a rule not only imposed by my parents but also his parents. I was a good Italian girl and it was not to be tolerated. If we did, we would definitely not be showing the family and the community our good family values and morals. I had a curfew to abide by, there was no sleeping over each other's houses even on the couch or staying late in the night alone and no travel: local or overseas.

As I write this, I can recall that when we would hang out together it was often simply watching TV at our respective homes. We would be either in the lounge with other family members or as John had a TV in his room we would hang on top of his single bed and if so, the door always had to remain wide open. This simple thing was showing respect to our parents and siblings and they regularly walked past to casually ask if we wanted a drink or something. How times have changed! Now my 15-year-old son requests that when he entertains his friends, we allow them the privacy to talk freely without parents hanging around. My husband and I give him that respect and privacy in our home with his friends and we disappear to another room. No open door and constant checking policy implemented with his friends. I feel we are more mindful of the peer group pressure that we went through and that our parents dismissed as unimportant.

Initially I thought that because we had only started dating that it may change further down the track. No, not in the slightest. A few years later when it was firmly established that we were a couple, we were attending all family functions together including family weddings, and were thinking of travelling to the USA on discounted tickets we had available to us. I asked my mum. She responded with: "I am not sure. Probably no, but I will discuss with your dad." John asked his mum and it was a definite "No. And no travelling together until you're married just to make it clear." We do not want people to talk badly about you and our family was the reason. *OMG please* I thought. What a load of ethnic rules crap! As if ethnic people of my generation had not travelled together previously. As a result of this parental negativity we decided to do the right thing and wait. I waited and waited and waited for 8 entire years before we finally went away on our honeymoon overseas to discover the world together (and of course visit the other ethnic family relatives on the other side of the world while we were there).

In comparison, my sisters who were still single and not partnered could travel where they wanted and all three of them travelled overseas on working holidays for several years before they returned to resettle in Adelaide. By this time my dad had relaxed the rules and decided if they were not partnered by the time they were in their mid 20's then they were in fact able to travel and come and go from the family home. We always knew that we would be welcomed home if we needed a place to live, no matter our age. So that's what my sisters did. All the while, their sister Claudia stayed home, waiting for her day to come when she would walk down that red carpeted church aisle and then receive permission to travel the world with her husband.

This restriction I felt was one of those expectations that was antiquated and depressing. I felt very much again in a box while I waited. When I felt the need to escape the confines of Adelaide and the travel rules, I would head off solo or with my sisters and girlfriends to see parts of the world for the both of us for a few weeks at a time, and John would head interstate with his friends on regular boys' football and soccer trips.

Some of my favourite short trips were to Melbourne to visit my Giussa girlfriend, Gabi. She had moved to Melbourne after our time at university for a new and exciting job role in fashion buying. She lived off Chapel Street in a cute villa surrounded by fashion outlets, restaurants and bars. We spoke often and she said that I was always welcome to stay with her if needed a short getaway from Adelaide. That is exactly what I did every year for about 4 years until she moved to Sydney. I would land on her doorstep for a few days or a week and we would enjoy our Giussa time together, connecting along with shopping trips, restaurants, the art gallery, theatre and different sightseeing adventures around Melbourne. It was a great escape from my parents' home and I felt that I was still being adventurous. I loved spending time with my fellow Giussa, the moment we reconnected it felt like the good old days at university. Then I would return to Adelaide, where John would pick me up at the airport. I would get off the plane fully loaded with my shopping bags and adventure stories, all happy and ready to go back to home life and work. I am so grateful for that initial soul sister Giussa connection with Gabi and our ongoing friendship and support still to this day despite her relocation to Auckland in New Zealand. Once you have a Giussa bond, you will always have the bond for life.

It was fortunate that John came from the same Italian culture as me and that we both loved and respected our parents. Therefore we didn't want to upset them by disrespecting the cultural rules and create talk amongst the family members. If we had not been two young ethnics facing this together I am not sure any other boyfriend or girlfriend would have been as supportive: especially the long lead up to getting married. The reality was that people got married quickly due to this restrictive rule. Many ethnic girls would comment that they got married to get out of the house and away from their strict parents' rules about everything they did.

This rule also extended to my staying home with my parents until I entered my marital home. This was despite the fact that John and I had both invested together and purchased a home and had a joint mortgage four years before we were married. The rent money helped us with the mortgage expenses. The only upside of this scenario was the fact our ethnic parents do not charge their children rent or living expenses, and so I was able to save my money for my wedding costs and also save for our home renovations. Despite this financial help if I had my time again I would have moved into that house immediately after settlement - married or not married - and have the opportunity to have my own space.

Looking back now, this scenario would be one of the first things I would have changed. I wish I had the courage to say that "this is what we want to do with our time together as a couple," and travel or move in together earlier. The reality is that we should have married a lot sooner as the wait time had a flow on effect to starting a family when we finally got married. A definite sliding door moment in life.

I now feel that waiting for the right time to do things and being ready for the next step in life is not a great plan. The reality is there is never the right time to change and you cannot control what happens in your life and there is never a right time for things.

Getting Married to an Australian-Italian Boy

I loved getting married and planning my wedding was one of the most exciting and creative times of my life. I couldn't wait for the day to finally come together and experience the event.

I had tried to intertwine the traditional ethnic elements into our wedding day. I may have felt that the unwritten rules were unjust within my life however, I also loved many Italian traditions and the meaning behind them. I went to the extent of researching why things were done in a specific way and tried to implement the tradition. For example, I discovered that the sugared almonds one would receive in the bonbonniere from weddings was a symbol of fertility for the wedding couple. You must have odd numbers (either 3 or 5) of sugared almonds placed in a material cloth and attached to the item you were gifting. I became fascinated by the tradition of all things. I wanted to implement the traditional aspects of our culture but with more of a modern feel that followed a colour theme and style. I had love quotes on the individualised invitation that I designed with a graphic designer. Our love and hearts theme was then carried through to the hall table displays, flowers and the love heart bonbonniere that I had designed and assembled with my bridesmaids. It was a very stressful time as well as an exciting one:

we were also trying to please the parents who were paying for part of the wedding, and incorporate our wishes as a couple.

My parents were easy going about the wedding planning and allowed me to co-ordinate most things. They simply provided me with their list of family and friends they wanted to attend and a budget they had allocated for the wedding day, which included the reception and bridal dress requirements. I laugh now as I write this as I approached the event in a different way to a majority of other brides. I was in a finance role at the time, so I asked my parents what their budget was and they received a detailed itemised expenses listing in return. I shopped around for quotes and worked within my budget, including the wedding dress and associated expenses. My parents were not wealthy and they worked hard all their lives to provide for their family and support us throughout our lives. My approach was not from a perspective of "this is what I want and what I must have and I do not care how much it costs." I respected that I was one of four girls in my family and despite being the first to marry; whatever they provided to me must also be provided to my sisters when their time came to walk down the aisle. I was also mindful and grateful that they were helping me financially for my part of the wedding day and my planning respected that.

Like all ethnic parents, both sides were mainly concerned with the reception venue and catering of good Italian food served to our family and friends, as well as ensuring we followed the traditional sequence of things on the day. My in-laws helped us negotiate the pricing and food selection at a local Italian wedding venue called

John Di Fede that they had hired for their daughter's wedding the year prior. Although this was not my first choice of wedding venues, I was also mindful of their right to be part of this decision along with my parents as they were also assisting us as a couple to pay for the reception. In the Italian community there are distinct rules and traditions on who pays for what aspect of the day and who is part of the decision-making process. The rules include the fact that the female has the right to choose the church and the groom's parents host the day after BBQ event at their home where you all gather again the next day to open the gifts and count the envelopes received ('Buste'). Furthermore, yes, we do write down what people have gifted us in the wedding cards (I still have mine kept in a drawer to this day). The kitchen tea and hen's night which includes both sides of the family is co-ordinated with the bride by the bridesmaids.

In the end we had 290 guests in total: 100 from John's side, 100 mutual friends and 90 from my parents' side. This amazingly was a standard number of wedding guests at weddings we were attending for mutual friends that year. We were also fortunate enough to have some overseas guests from the USA, Belgium and Switzerland, as well as 20 guests from interstate.

I always remember my dad's nervousness and excitement at walking me down the aisle in our family church. His third daughter was finally getting married and the first of his four daughters. He was probably thinking "WHOOP WHOOP, we made it to the church and her husband can worry about her now." I'm sure he was also thinking his daughter would of course listen to her new husband the rest of her life like the good ethnic girl he raised and nurtured on the right path in life.

There is a time when you reach the end of the church aisle and your dad moves aside and gives your hand to your future partner - like a relay race baton exchanged to the next male influence in your life. It is like you have been carefully cared for by one person and now it is time to be passed on to another and together you will win the race of life. I remember looking back at my dad and had a sudden feeling how things in life would now dramatically change based on this simple exchange.

He knew at that moment that he no longer had any control over my decisions moving forward and it was my husband (in my dad's mind) who had the final say.

Laugh out loud dad, of course we will listen to each other as we are equal partners in life. Hmm, how naive I really was at this age. I don't think equal say with your parents and husband actually exists in our culture, despite how old you are in this world.

One of the funniest aspects of the planning was my absolute determination not to just sway dance to our bridal song like I had seen at other weddings. I wanted a fully choreographed 'Dancing with the Stars' dance routine.

We enlisted a dancing teacher to help us achieve this goal with not only one song but two meaningful tunes. The first was a jazz song by Ella Fitzgerald "Cheek to Cheek" as soon as we walked in and cut the traditional entrance ribbon. I remembered the song chosen fondly for its meaningful lyrics:

"I'm in heaven and my heart beats so that I can hardly speak and I seem to find the happiness I seek, when we are out together dancing cheek to cheek."

I have never managed to get John back to dancing lessons again since that time but for ten weeks leading up to our wedding, he attended lessons with me every week and he practised and danced with the male teacher hand in hand to get it right. Bless him and his dedication to my bridal dance dream. We were a definite hit on that dance floor. I must admit that despite forgetting some of the steps on the day my new husband sure can dip me like a pro dancer.

I realised that I had grown up with all these wedding traditions and there was a procedure of things at all ethnic weddings that you experienced over the years. I wanted the same traditions but only jazzed up and elegant with the ethnic portions toned down a tad.

On the night we had a great band playing both traditional Italian songs and contemporary songs. We arrived in beautiful Cadillac cars and drank champagne on the way to the city park for the obligatory family photos and wedding party shots around the city of Adelaide prior to the reception.

In the end we still incorporated most traditions. They included the receiving line and personally greeting all our guests with our parents into the reception centre, the speeches, the first dance streamers wrap and the final departure chain that guests form to wish the couple good luck on their journey as a married couple. The only aspect I was adamant not to include was the dried ice buckets used to create ambience for the bridal dance. Instead, we performed our dance routine and created our own magical effect.

Being Accepted by Your Future Husband's Family

This is such a big subject amongst my fellow ethnic females, but it is a hard thing to discuss - and especially write about - without being seen as disrespectful. Essentially their influence is for the rest of your life and your children's life and you always want to be able to connect with your family members forever.

Your new family, including extended family members, will form part of the heritage that you develop within your new family as a couple and will also influence your children. They are the link between you and your parents as a married couple and then that translates to your children, their grandchildren and the legacy of your families lives on through every merged element. No two families are the same. You may have been raised with the same values within the Italian community, however the reality is that you are raised by different parents and have different sibling relationships. I grew up with all sisters and John grew up with both genders in his family. Despite the struggles and the differences in way things were done, you are essentially brought up to be loyal to your parents and siblings - no matter what - and this is the same for your husband's family.

My mother saw me about to travel the same path she had also taken as a young 18-year-old bride. I was entering a world where I would continue to have to play by more unwritten rules and other people's expectations of me and be judged by these rules. My mother advised me when I became part of and eventually married into another Italian family, "You are now part of their family and they are your first priority over even us, your own parents." My mum stated that I must try to put them first and follow their family rules. It was important for them to be happy with my behaviour and for me to be respectful at all times, even if I didn't agree with them. "Your husband's wellbeing is your first priority and his parents and family's acceptance of you and their happiness are just as important." I think she was trying to tell me I represented not only my family values but theirs as well, and to always be mindful of that responsibility.

Reflecting back I now notice that there was no talk of self-worth or self-care and putting your needs first. Our generation of women were taught to put others first and ourselves last and be as humble as possible with our own achievements in life. Our kids and husbands came before ourselves and our careers. It is the ethnic way, the selfless mother who is exhausted to her core yet still has the courage to not give up: even when she has nothing left.

This very selfless trait has been passed on to our generation of women born in the 1960's and 70's from our selfless mothers. However, we do not have the same circumstances or environment as our immigrant mothers: our environment holds different types of pressures. This has resulted in the creation of many selfless, but guilt-ridden, ethnic daughters. I was one of those daughters and daughters-in-law trying to work through all the expectations placed on me. We were trying to achieve what our mothers did at home, meet the expectations of our husbands brought up by another selfless mother, meet our new generation children's needs, meet the new in-laws' expectations and then our own career pressures and work commitments and then finally our own life expectations and dreams.

Our mothers' expectations of their own careers in Australia were not very high as they knew in their hearts that they simply needed to work and provide for the family. My mother's focus was on our schooling and meeting those private school fees for her four daughters. This dedication to our future and schooling then set up my own expectations of my career at a higher level. My parents were proud that their daughter could aspire higher than what they were able to. Yet I was also expected to achieve all the other role expectations as well, and was judged when I found it difficult to juggle all the roles as a daughter.

Fortunately for the sake of our parents, husbands and children, we ethnic women are very good at keeping the peace. This is a phrase we repeat to ourselves often and out loud. We follow the unwritten rules of not making comments to ensure we are not disrespectful to anyone and to go with the flow, especially in a new family environment. In reality, openly arguing with family members is often avoided and, on some occasions, what is not being said is just as bad as what is being said out loud. I feel that our culture is not very good at calm discussions and many things are expressed with heightened emotion. "Sweeping things under the carpet" is quite normal practice within our families. Yet the judgement is still there, sitting unresolved for years, sometimes even the rest of our lives.

Challenging and arguing with family members is not encouraged; we act and are respectful to each other. This is probably why a lot of marriages are saved and big ethnic families are still gathering together.

Our Italian culture is also underpinned by our Catholic faith and religion. This means we try to see the good in people and not create discord, as there is a universal understanding that the final judgement will always be by God in heaven.

In a perfect world, we as daughters should not have to be told how to conform or how to act within any family. We should be proud of ourselves and be accepted for who we are. We should be able to speak our truth always. This is in fact the way the new female generation are. In some ways I envy them, yet they have also lost the focus on 'family first' with more an emphasis on 'myself first', which results in some family disconnection. I am not sure which is the better way personally.

My in-laws and their large extended family members are good people and they welcomed me with open arms into their home and lives. John and I met at a very young age: only 21 years old. I felt that his parents thought it was therefore their role to guide us both in the right direction. We accepted this guidance openly; however I think they felt they needed to do this for the rest of our lives unfortunately. I do not think ethnic parents know when to draw the line in terms of when to guide through their opinion and when to stop. It is as if once you allow their opinion to be accepted it is also for the rest of your life. I stepped away from my parent's opinion briefly and tried to guide myself in the world only to land back in the same level of expectation from another family.

I was a confident and happy individual who finally got married at 29 years old after waiting patiently for eight years at home with my parents until I was able to walk down the church aisle and live in my own home with my husband. We were finally in our own home together and I believed that our lives were ours to decide on as to where we went and what we did on an ongoing basis. How naive I was!

As I have matured, I now realise that family interactions are never straightforward and each family has judgements and triggers for their behaviour. Our heritage and own unique environments will always play a part in the way we think and act and obligations are all tied up within this complex merge of emotions. In my first year of marriage I hosted both sides of the family for Christmas, Easter and several large birthday events. We had a home now and all of a sudden I was required to be this experienced caterer and take over some of the family hosting obligations: to step up and give back to the family. Luckily I love co-ordinating functions and despite my limited cooking skills I managed to achieve some beautifully catered functions with all of the traditional food and my own speciality: beautifully co-ordinated themed table settings. I also learnt a new unwritten rule thanks to my Neapolitan great aunty during my first year of marriage. Every time I saw her at my parents' home (which was regularly) I reminded her that she was welcome to pop in and visit us anytime. I was told by my great aunty that it was my obligation to officially invite all my aunties and uncles over separately, to officially welcome them to my new home in my first year of marriage. Her simply dropping in without the official invitation by the married couple was not being respectful. Needless to say, I was annoyed by this unwritten rule, hence her official invitation to visit came after my first year of marriage and only after the constant nagging by my dad. "Oh my God dad do we have to make it such a formal and official thing? Why is this necessary?" I would complain. His response was: "Just be respectful Claudia, organising an afternoon coffee visit will not kill you. Your aunty and uncle sponsored us to migrate to Australia and they are important family members. So is your godmother and all the aunties and uncles on John's side. Regularly visiting them in their homes and inviting them over is a sign of respect. This is the expectation we and your in-laws have of you now that you are married in your own home. It is simply the Italian way and the way we raised you to be."

The pressure was real, along with the guilt. I would follow this tradition and still do; however, I am now more willing to stay connected with the older generation rather than seeing it as an obligation. John has had a big positive influence in this area of my life. He especially loves visiting his relatives and cousins and was more fortunate than myself in having an extensive family surrounding him growing up. His memories with his family and cousins are filled with treasured times and laughter. While we juggle a hectic life we both make time, especially at Christmas and

Easter. The connection to his older family members is one that he treasures, particularly their stories of moving to Australia and their wisdom that they impart on our generation. This connection is respect in his eyes, as well as connections to his heritage. It's not about the percolated coffee and biscotti that are served at the visit. The visit is showing love and telling that person that they are important in your world and they mean something. This older generation also appreciate the effort taken by our generation and especially light up when they see our children come as well. It is the Italian way, and shows manners, just like giving them a kiss and hug when you see them. It is a tradition that displays love and respect. It is also something that we both instil in our son, yet we have changed in that we do not try to force the obligation on him, we simply explain why it is important for him to take part in this cultural display of love and emotion.

During my married life, I had to conform and adapt according to the unwritten ethnic rules to fit in the box that was expected of me in my new family. This was also the same for many of my girlfriends. It wasn't an unusual situation to be part of. The truth of the matter was that there was now another family and a whole new rule book I had to understand as a married person without any directions or guidance. I was left working it out alone and subsequently made many mistakes along the way. I often felt I was doing the dog paddle in unchartered ocean waters. At times there were many regretful compromises and many times I lost myself in the process of trying to fit in.

One of the best traditions we had with my husband's family were the weekly family dinners at my in-laws' house. All four children, their partners and any children would turn up after work on a nominated night each week. It was referred to as the in-law dinner night. This was a traditional thing many Italian families did to ensure that despite our busy lives and jobs we gathered as a family and shared a meal together. At the end of the night after three courses and coffee we all left for our own homes filled to the brim with delicious rustic Italian food, along with a few containers of leftovers for lunch the next day.

This tradition lasted about 10 years with my in-laws and it was a great testimony to their values and determination to keep us all connected as a family and to each other as we grew older and more children entered the family. Unfortunately this tradition stopped when my mother in-law did not have the energy to maintain the meal preparation due to her illness. She was the family rock and was instrumental in keeping everyone together. Sadly my son and her other grandchildren will also miss out on this amazing tradition and wonderful rustic food they both prepared all day together to present to their children for dinner.

Despite the enjoyable times we had together at weekly dinners and special birthday events, I always managed to miss the cue for the time I had to get up from the table and help serve the next course or start washing the dishes. I was usually the one making table conversation while John's sisters moved swiftly to the kitchen like a lightning bolt at the right moment. Of course they knew the signs to look for as they had been doing this role since they were born with their mothers. It was like the last crumb had been eaten from the person's plate and *swoosh* you were up and ready to get the next thing served or the dishes washed. The men always remained in their seats at the table conversing, while the women got up. In their eyes conversation was not as important as the serving of the meal and cleaning up. Once this was done then the females were then able to relax for the night. On regular occasions I would get the reminder to stop talking and help the girls and that the 'sparra' (tea towel) was waiting for me to use.

In comparison I came from a family of girls and we were all treated equally and took turns in helping our mother with the dinner and dishes. We were not required to all be in the kitchen together to show our respect as a united female front serving the family.

In retrospect maybe the challenge for me was how to find the right balance of meeting the cultural expectations of my in-laws, remain respectful and still feel like my presence was more important than just providing labour in the kitchen. I felt like my voice at the table was just as important as the male voices and should not necessarily be shut down because there were dishes to be cleared and more courses to serve. That was something I battled with internally as once again I was forced back into that box – the very box I had been trying so hard to bust out of and I thought marriage would allow me to do.

I must acknowledge that I know this regular reminder of my role, along with their daughters, came from a place of love by my in-laws. They loved their daughters and regarded them as just as important as their sons. Their daughter-in-law and son-in-law were also important members and loved. Being included and loved was never in question from my perspective. It was simply the Italian way - their way - and the cultural rules they followed as children and their expectations of their own children. They simply didn't understand my personal resistance to it all and that the approach they took with me felt very controlling.

Even though the men would simply sit at the table at their positions and allow the women to co-ordinate the food, collect the plates, serve and do the dishes, it wasn't as if the men were lazy individuals. My father-in-law worked very hard to support his family. He had a milk distribution business his entire work life and his son - my husband - had been helping him deliver milk to the neighbourhood since he was 12 years old until he started his own busy career. They were in fact hard working men with a strong work ethic and supporting their families financially weighed very heavily on their shoulders, just as was the case with my own dad. It was again the way it was and the predefined roles that they all were used to and simply accepted as part of life.

From another perspective, I found Italian kitchens are where all the action is and the ethnic women come alive and connect in this space. This is also where all the family gossip gets whispered to you as they pass along the plate to dry. The washing and drying task required to be carried out by the women may seem very primitive but I have also had the most interesting conversations and connections with women in the kitchen doing the dishes. I suppose it's a bit like a women's circle working together, connecting and getting the task done using our unique skills.

Another quite funny incident I experienced was my surname changeover. In ethnic families once you walk down that church aisle you sign the marriage certificate and then 'bang!' Like magic, the surname you had your entire life is wiped out and replaced with a new one. Changing your name on documents takes time, however for some reason I was constantly asked by my new extended family if I was going to change my name over to my new surname. I actually never had an issue with changing my name over; I waited eight years for my wedding day and I always anticipated to change my surname. I was just stunned with the questioning and the testing of my level of commitment to the family name or whether I would really conform. So my name was hyphenated for about 6 months as Di Martino–Callisto until my driver's licence came up for renewal and the double barrel name was changed quietly and without judgement and fuss. I did feel sorry for my dad that his family name would be lost forever as his brother didn't have sons either. Such a small thing made into such a big issue! This is also the Italian way unfortunately.

In comparison to my sisters who were also born into the same Italian family, many of my experiences and obligations that were part of our culture were uniquely mine. They all married non-ethnics and they didn't have all the layered rulings and obligations like myself. My sisters often remarked that they got off lightly with all that traditional Italian stuff compared to me, as they only had to deal with the expectations imposed by our parents. Gratefully they supported me as much as they could and were my anchors. This was especially true when I experienced infertility and undertook 5 years of IVF treatment, where they visually saw me crumble under my own and the cultural pressure. During this time, I simply felt I was not able to discuss these areas of failure in my life with most of my other family members and within the community. Another part of the Italian way: never tell anyone your deepest level of pain and failures in life and always put on a smile through the pain and a brave face. Italians are resilient people and sometimes talking about truth and deep emotions and sharing that emotion is often not encouraged. Being silent about personal pain and suffering is the norm. Another strong immigrant trait imposed on us during our childhood. Something I feel definitely needs to change within our community and families.

Infertility and Being an Ethnic Woman

When you fail to achieve a successful pregnancy year after year, you fail in your role as an ethnic wife.

No matter what your friends and husband tell you in regard to not achieving a pregnancy and how understanding they are. You have in fact failed to meet the basic requirement within the cultural family and community expectations. It is the truth according to the ethnic rule book of good girls' expectations and behaviours. This cultural understanding and unspoken knowledge cuts deeply when you're facing a future without children. It cuts deeper than anyone could ever guess. Creating a family is one of the main reasons why people marry and I had already waited eight long years to get to that stage in my life. The feeling of failure in this area is immense on so many levels. It is rarely spoken of, but those born ethnic know these heartless facts. It is a universal feeling that as a woman you are challenged by the fact that you are not able to do something you are biologically made for. As a wife you are challenged by the fact that you cannot give your husband an heir or a legacy. The cold hard fact is that you will be always on the back foot as you have not provided any grandchildren. This is the unspoken truth. It is the internal pain that I faced. It is the ongoing pain that stopped me living my full life.

After many years of sadness, I was grateful to give birth to my son Marcus at the age of 38, after achieving a successful IUI treatment with a fertility specialist clinic. I had been married to my husband from the age of 29 years old and had experienced infertility for a long time, until I desperately decided to seek fertility assistance in my late 30's. After having my son, at the age of 40 I returned to the fertility clinic with the hope of having another baby. I underwent IVF treatment for a further 5 years with no success.

The feeling of isolation and of failure combined with the lack of empathy from those around you is very difficult to accept and overcome. I had such hopes and dreams of the IVF treatment being successful that my sense of self and identity became intrinsically attached to the outcome of having another child.

During this long, difficult time I discovered that it is important to protect your own feelings and try not to overanalyse every situation or comment. If you cannot go to one more family or friends' happy event or birthday, do not go. If you feel sad, allow yourself the space to face those feelings and feel them, as they will pass. In reality many family and friends are simply not equipped to give advice or be empathetic during this journey. I became very disillusioned and disappointed with friends and family and the entire human race during this time. This feeling, combined with the fact IVF is not spoken about openly and there is an underlying stigma attached to it, made me feel that no one really cared.

Being of Italian heritage, I also struggled with comments and expectations to have one child after another, and that I was being selfish to only choose to have one child. Little did they know that I was in fact trying my very best to expand my family. There was also the misunderstanding by many that only having one child was easier than raising two or more children. I regularly heard from other mothers: "Oh, you only have one child, it should be easy for you to juggle everything in life."

In my darkest day of undergoing IVF treatments I could not do it anymore. By the fifth year after stopping and starting cycles with a total of 6 rounds during this time, I simply didn't have the strength to stop crying and continue on with the planning, the schedule, the blood tests, the injections, the clinic visits and egg retrieval operations, coupled with the high anxiety that developed and the sleepless nights going over every detail and analysing every feeling in my body. Let alone trying to work at my hectic job and juggling mortgage payments and saving for the financial burden of the treatments.

At the same time I was also raising my beautifully sensitive and clingy toddler Marcus; I was trying to be a supportive wife, daughter, sister and friend. All the while pretending to the world around me that I was ok. I had mastered the art of the fake smile and pretending to be a happy dynamic individual (my former self). The reality was that my silence created a huge inner sadness; people rarely asked if I was doing ok and it literally felt like my soul was being ripped apart. I just kept telling myself I was a tough ethnic chick and I could DO THIS.

YOU'VE GOT THIS Claude!

The unfortunate truth is that I didn't have boundless energy and underneath that smiling façade I was barely keeping it together emotionally.

Undergoing IVF was the start of life passing through a long tunnel of darkness that made me feel that I would never see the light again. In reality there are no tunnels without exits. Although at the time, I never felt that I could possibly find an exit or even think about exiting the IVF road and tunnel without achieving my outcome of having another child in my arms. Sadly, when I finally did exit that road at the age of 46, I came to realise and accept that there are some things I cannot achieve, no matter how hard I try. I also slowly realised after all those years that there is life and joy once you stop and stand still for a while. There is an end of the road in all things and life does go on: one can be happy again and grateful for the life they have.

My heart goes out to all those couples trying to conceive who have not achieved motherhood/parenthood. Please be kind to yourself. **You are valued**, and your life will be exceptional: with or without children.

I now recognise that I had little control over the process and I should really have released control to help myself. IVF is an emotional and difficult program of treatment. Ultimately, by changing my mindset to become more emotionally resilient; my emotional stress healed and made me a stronger person.

Letting go of my thoughts throughout the process was tough; surrendering to a feeling when that feeling is sadness and loss of hope that you will achieve your dream is a difficult thing. However at some point that feeling eventually subsided and I was simply grateful that I in fact had many things in life to be thankful for: particularly my one child, Marcus.

My son Marcus was a little toddler at the time when I started calling him my 'Shining Light'. He simply wanted his mum be to present and give him attention and over time because of his constant laughs and smiles the darkness of the tunnel was subsiding and the sun was shining again. I could see the light shining in a different way and I knew it was time to move on to other dreams. It wasn't failure, it was just a different path in life.

From this heartache has grown a labour of love – a business Shining Light, which I established with my sister Diana, who also endured many years of IVF.

The emotions which accompany the infertility journey were very overwhelming and difficult at times, however through the use of journals and positive affirmations that we both adopted, we were able to believe that we had the inner strength to overcome any challenge life threw at us.

Shining Light aims to inspire all women and children to be grateful, positive, resilient and kind through the sale of gratitude journals, affirmation cards and motivational products.

You can find out more here:

www.shininglightcd.com.au
Facebook.com/Shining Light.cd
Instagram @Shininglight.cd

The Ethnic Girls' Career Options

That refusal to be placed in a pre-determined ethnic girl box gave me the strength to align with who I really was as a person in my professional life. Being my corporate self in the workplace and not just a good Italian girl gave me courage in this part of my life and I subsequently dreamed big after finishing my university business course and set high goals of achievement.

I will be honest and say that I have felt workplace discrimination in a very subtle form most of my career. I was an ambitious female working in a lot of male-dominated work environments. Firstly, I was a confident woman and secondly, I was ethnic: most people assumed I would have kids and give up my career to stay home and look after them.

I believe that everyone should have a choice in life to work or raise children or do a combination of both. There should be no judgement on what path a woman chooses is right for herself or her family's needs. Men are never questioned or even need to make that decision, let alone have a discussion at interview stage about what their marital status is or future family plans are, nor do they need to keep it secret for fear of discrimination.

Although it is now against the law to ask these types of questions at a job interview or in the workplace, I can still recall at various interviews being asked about my marital status and family planning in a very roundabout way, especially after being married and into my mid 30's. My thoughts were that they were always trying to assess if maternity leave would be taken sooner rather than later and whether I was I worth hiring and developing my skills, especially if it was for a management role. On these occasions I always played down any discussions on children and redirected the conversation to my career ambitions. I would get frustrated by this questioning and felt I could never really be open and be my true authentic self and make mention of my background and family. There was such judgement by both women and men interviewing at that time.

Once I finished university I started as a graduate at the ANZ Bank in 1990. At this time the banking system was not very progressive and very male orientated. My graduate program started in a city branch learning the role of a teller and then assistant lender to the branch manager. My first role also required me to make coffees for my branch manager every morning. As you can imagine, I was not very impressed with this coffee making role for my male non-ethnic older manager.

Oh my God, I just worked so hard at university to achieve a degree and you're telling me I have to serve you coffee like I do at home?

I spent 5 years working within the ANZ Bank and my last role with the organisation was as their customer service manager and internal marketing. I was 25 years old at the time. I felt so proud of my first management role: I was managing a team of two staff members and working with all the senior managers of the business in the Adelaide Metro area. I loved the role but when they announced a restructure of my area back to the head marketing department in Melbourne and they were re-allocating me to another department, I decided to leave the bank and try to expand my skills in sales and marketing in other roles (much to the disappointment of my father).

My father could not believe that I would leave and risk the safe and secure nature of the bank to simply try something else. "Why? You have a good job for life at the bank!" The shoe was now on the other foot and he was asking why? I didn't change jobs because I wanted to upset my parents; I simply was restless with my past and present life being defined to a single path.

My parents were hard workers and they remained in their first job since migrating to Australia. Consistency, hard work and dedication to one employer for life was seen a valued skill in their eyes. They steadfastly believed this, even though the hard physical work my dad undertook at the factory for over 25 years, left him with industrial deafness and swollen hands from the fine manual handling.

I didn't want to live my life in that way. I pursued higher education and worked hard to achieve in my studies despite the difficulties and the judgement I faced. I was not willing to stay on the same employment path for my remaining career simply because it was safe and stable.

I decided that my career and job roles were my own decision to make and my desire to see what else the world could offer me was providing me the courage to simply try. Some job changes have not been successful and I did not enjoy them. I usually moved on after giving the role at least 12 months.

During my 20's and 30's I actively changed my jobs and industry to push myself forward in unchartered territory and go after things I wanted to achieve in life. I was adamant to experience as much as possible in the corporate world. I achieved this through additional studies in management, training development and then building and construction. I was fighting this restlessness inside myself while waiting to start my married life that I used this energy to pursue my career and study and learn as much as I could in areas that interested me.

For many years in all of the job roles I had in finance, sales, marketing and training development prior to children, I made a conscious effort of not disclosing my background and talking about my family and cultural activities to mask the other side of my ethnic life. I was simply Australian born and raised, and schooled in Adelaide at a girl's private school. The moment I would tell others in the workplace and open up about family life and even my weekend activities, I would feel the judgement even about simple things like being responsible for the cleaning, cooking and meal preparation. For example, some of the comments included: "I get my husband to help with all the household tasks, I'm not his slave. But that's what your culture is like, you women serve your men folk and do everything for your kids."

"Yes, well you are right. We do a lot for our families, and my mum did that for me as well. But technically I do not work on any areas outside like gardening: that is my husband's responsibility." It was at these times when you were explaining things that you realised that you both had just carried on the clearly defined roles that your parents did when you were growing up. Not all comments were negative, though. There were lots of positive comments about the amazing food that Italians prepared and how lucky we were to be skilled in cooking these rustic foods. I felt that Italian food was now seen as trendy and this element many people were suddenly able to connect with. It was a shame that I actually wasn't a confident or experimental cook. I cooked what I knew from my mum and mother-in-law. Recipes taught visually and methods used from generation to generation.

I had another pivotal life changing moment at the age of 36. At the time I was actively running training programs for women to re-enter the workforce after their children had started school. I was empowering all these female clients to achieve their next goals in life and reassess what their next career goal would be in life outside having a family. All the while I was experiencing infertility and not able to get pregnant to achieve my own family goal. I would start my training off with defining what short and long-term goals were and in fact that long-term goals could relate to something completely different and that it was important to focus on taking measured short-term steps towards your current goals and have your bigger picture - whatever that may be - as your final destination. I would say: "Come on, let's start writing down and aspiring to your dreams, no dream is too big or too grand." My own personal example to the group was my long-term goal to renovate and flip houses for profit one day after I moved on from training and development.

There was a real irony in that time of my life. I was in fact trying to achieve what they had achieved and they were trying to achieve the workplace confidence and success I was having in life. I'm not sure if the delivery of this training at this point in my life was the universe trying to telling me to stop feeling depressed and do something about my own situation and family dreams and goals.

I was getting worried that my life plan was not happening and I was possibly facing life without children. At the time my sister asked me, "what are your other dreams in life outside having a child?" I responded by saying that I always dreamed of renovating and flipping homes for profit. She stated "Well, what are you waiting for? Stop putting your life on hold. Live it now!"

So that's I what I did. I moved my long-term plan up and made it my short-term plan, then set out to achieve it.

I am not sure why I was always drawn to male dominated environments such as the construction industry. I had actively renovated our home and simply loved the experience and achievement from repurposing something old to something new. I loved building form and structure and had a genuine passion to be a part of the industry. After a few weeks I commenced a certificate in Building with the Master Builders Association and began my search for the project house to renovate.

Studying the building course was very challenging and technical, however I simply loved learning all the jargon and the building process. I was of course the only female attending the class and the other male participants didn't interact very much with me initially until they learned that my training experience meant I had great skills in writing up the group discussion work and presenting it at the front of class for the group. Then I was welcomed into any male group I was sitting next to in class moving forward. Twelve months later I had completed my building course, specialising in contract administration, and obtained a job in the building industry as a contracts administrator with a commercial builder. I was so proud of my Giussa self that I had achieved this career milestone and was persistent in finishing my training despite the struggles of initially not understanding a lot of the content and having to study harder due to never working on a building site.

Over that twelve month period I had also completed the renovated home project with the assistance of my husband and sub-contractors. It was with much happiness and sadness that we sold the property a month before I gave birth to my child for a reasonable profit. My goal had been achieved despite the challenges.

WOO HOO, this Giussa was on fire!

My electrician friend Carmine who rewired the project home for me at a very generous discount recently reminded me how much of a go-getter I have always been. He said: "Remember Claude, you were flipping houses even before flipping houses was a trendy thing to do. You should be very proud of this achievement in life." Bless you Carmine and thank you for the reminder.

The commercial building role was very rewarding and I was good at planning and documentation. Yet as soon as I advised my workplace that I was four months pregnant, my manager commenced making work life difficult. He openly advised me that I was no longer required to attend management meetings as he didn't see the point. I had decided that his discrimination and negativity was not going to affect my pregnancy or the job role that I enjoyed. I was a strong resilient Italian-raised corporate, experienced woman and no male manager was going to drive me away from the workplace. So, I simply put up with it. However "putting up with his behaviour" simply confirmed to him and the organisation that this type of discrimination towards a pregnant female within the workplace was ok.

Despite pushing through the remaining five months, I left that workplace 6 weeks before delivery as I simply couldn't stand the negativity and the stress was affecting my wellbeing. I was ecstatic to be having a child and I was grateful that I actually got pregnant at the age of 38. Unfortunately, my acceptance of this initial discrimination while pregnant did come back to have a bigger impact a few years later when I was again confronted by another male manager in the building industry with similar views.

I delivered Marcus in June 2005 and was very grateful that I *finally* now had my own little family and that I had managed to tick off a few bucket list dreams along the way.

Having sidestepped the children discussions most of my career I re-entered the building industry with a large Italian family business on a part-time basis after 12 months at home with my son.

At the age of 39 I was finally comfortable to discuss my background and family life as I was working with an entire organisation of other ethnic people. It felt very strange compared to the other organisations I had worked within, yet somehow I was strangely comfortable with being able to be my true ethnic friendly self and my ambitious career-focused self in the same space. It was as if the work mask was able to be removed and I could relax and enjoy it. It was a very loud, hectic place to work at with lots of friendly banter. We worked very hard for the organisation and there was a strong level of respect and teamwork. It was simply like one big ethnic family: everyone looked out for each other and we were all committed to the ongoing success of the businesses. Coffee was always free flowing as well as the laughter, connections and friendly slaps on the back.

The work standards and values of the business were established by an Italian migrant some 20 years prior. A very kind, customer focused and passionate man who gave many ethnic employees workplace opportunities. It wasn't simply a workplace team: it was a family. The upside of this working environment was that the ethnic values that we were brought up with also translated within this workplace and everyone knew what their expectations were, especially in regard to respect and hard work, as we all personally grew up with those traits. It was your hard work ethic that you were assessed and rewarded by. It was a very unique workplace and most individuals working there were second generation immigrant children like myself. Your hard work was rewarded with encouragement and it was a great inclusive family type team culture.

I had never experienced this type of strong workplace culture before and I have never again since leaving. This very culture is what many current large organisations aspire to: inclusion and diversity. Treating people as individuals and not just a number. No matter what our contribution and role, we all belonged and were seen as important.

During the four years I worked at this organisation, I worked with two great general managers who inspired and motivated their large production team and myself. Most importantly, my fellow female ethnic team members Anna and Mary were amazing to work with. Our connection and support of each other was unbreakable inside and outside of work. Despite the personal challenges I experienced, I consider myself fortunate to have left an organisation and still maintained a great group of friends who we refer to each other as "Comaras" and "Comparis". Any ethnic knows that if you're called this, you are special and considered family. I'm forever grateful for those laughs and connections we developed during that time and continue to enjoy to this day.

Despite this amazing teamwork there were a few problems I also faced within this work environment. The organisation had an old-fashioned management style. There were no female managers, only men. There were some very intelligent and efficient women that worked hard within this organisation but they had little opportunity to be promoted above their perceived value status. The role of ethnic women in their family or home had been carried over into this workplace and the women had no real choice but to accept it for what it was.

After about two years working there, I felt the workplace was generally supportive of working mothers. However, my immediate male supervisor believed that pregnant women were simply not of any value to the business long-term. Upon turning 40 I had decided to undertake IVF treatment to hopefully achieve another pregnancy. At the same time I overheard my male supervisor comment that another co-worker in the workplace wanted to be pregnant again. He stated that they would no longer consider her for any internal promotions as she would leave to have a baby and so there was no point in up-skilling her. This co-worker got pregnant two years later.

I was astounded by such obvious discrimination and that this was in fact workplace discrimination (not that he cared). During this same time frame I had a meeting with the male supervisor and was given a promotion to work with the project managers in a project support role. At the end of the discussion this same male supervisor advised me that the business was giving me a real opportunity to receive more responsibility and that now was not a time for me to "get pregnant." I was stunned and speechless. I remained silent and didn't respond at all. I couldn't believe it. I had this awful sinking feeling in my gut.

OMG here we go again, what is about me and the building industry and the issue of pregnancy. It is never about my hard work and performance? Always pregnancy.

As a result of his comment and my previous experience while pregnant at the other building company, I kept my IVF treatment plans to myself. I believed that it would only take at most one year to achieve another pregnancy. Little did I know at the time I was in for a difficult, soul crushing five-year journey.

This decision not to speak up within the workplace and again simply put up with the discrimination was probably the worst thing I could have done for my own wellbeing. However, at the time I simply did not want a repeat episode of what happened and the negativity and game playing by another person I was reporting to.

Two years later when my co-worker did get pregnant and I was still struggling with IVF, the same male supervisor decided that she could have a lighter workload as in his view her brain would stop fully functioning during pregnancy. So he off loaded some of her work to me. I was already under work pressure and dealing with the failure of IVF treatments (not that I could tell him that now two years later). The co-worker rejoiced that her workload was easier and she was able to relax during her remaining six months. She didn't care that another co-worker would be stressed and that it was unfair to all women to assume that pregnancy affected work efficiency. *Were we still in the dark ages with this type of behaviour?* It has always been hard climbing the corporate ladder with equal rights and equal pay for the same role and skill level, particularly in the building industry. I assumed that all women felt that they needed to work together in the workplace to achieve success and support each other and prevent discrimination from occurring. We need to be sisters in arms together. Obviously not in her eyes.

I haven't really nailed down why I was targeted for discrimination on the very difficult subject of pregnancy or trying to get pregnant. It wasn't as if the two male managers who were being discriminatory were not husbands and they also had children of their own. That was often the things I wanted to say the most: "Hey if someone did this to your wife would you be upset for her? So why do it to someone else and completely ignore employment legislation? Do you do realise that this is workplace bullying?"

During my pregnancy with Marcus I experienced a high level of stress and internal pain as a result of trying to work and be pregnant and the fear that something would go wrong. Then the second time around I was stressed hiding my treatments from everyone I worked with for years. This simple masking of my true feelings caused much grief and darkness. These circumstances would be something that many people would not understand. I simply lost my voice in the world and had to internalise it. I grieved this the entire time.

Many noted that they would have simply left the workplace if it happened to them. In hindsight that is what I should have done. I should have not fought so hard and simply left and saved my mental health. I didn't come from a family of wealth and privilege. I am a working-class girl through and through brought up by immigrant parents, I believed that hard work is what matters the most in the workplace, not someone's personal agenda. I also work very hard for the money I earn. If I wasn't working then I couldn't afford to have a baby and stay home to care for him, or try and have another one. I felt myself very much on my own hamster wheel during that time of my life.

It is really not within our ethnic nature to stand up and protest within the workplace. As women we simply do not openly complain about unfair and unjust circumstances as we are brought up surrounded by them within our own families. We put up with them for the sake of our families, accepting that is simply the way it is within our culture. However, this in fact disadvantages us within the workplace. Males and non-ethnic women are so much better at calling out unfair and unjust practices and getting what they want and more, as they have not been conditioned their entire life to simply be quiet about their own needs or achievements.

Ethnic females are taught by our parents to wait to be acknowledged for our hard work. Self-promotion is frowned upon as a female including being aggressive and a go-getter. In my case, the waiting patiently for my acknowledgement in the workplace rarely happened. I was often left feeling frustrated as to why a less competent yet more self-promoting person was given an opportunity and not myself. It was simply because she was not afraid to ask for it and go and get it for herself and not really care about anyone else's feelings or situation but her own.

As one girlfriend stated to me recently, we never were allowed to 'Avanti' ourselves (put ourselves forward). We were always told to never brag about our achievements and how good we were and we were never as confident as what we should have really been. We ethnic females work hard, we deserve the recognition and high salaries yet we lack confidence in asking for that acknowledgement by others, especially our superiors. Sadly, some of us have also carried this selfless trait on to our children of this generation where they at times get left behind as we also frown on their confidence and self-promotion. We usually point out their negative traits first, rather than their positive traits, just like our parents did to us. We do not want showy children similar to what our parents believed, however I believe there is a difference between showy children and being confident in your skills and being proud to speak up about these great traits. This is where I believe we need to change not only for our children but for ourselves in the workplace and in life as ethnic females. It is never too late to start my fellow Giussas. Let's remember to 'Avanti' ourselves as we deserve it.

Working within the building industry suddenly became very difficult, especially hiding the effects of the difficult treatments. I often felt like my life was crashing down around me, even though I was putting on a brave face for the world. After a very difficult day at work and deciding that my supervisor was never going to give me the support I required, I decided to again change focus and work in an area that provided some work-life balance. I commenced studying accounting and bookkeeping. I had the intention of opening up my own bookkeeping practice and helping small businesses with their finance requirements, particularly subcontractors in the building industry. After a year of studying very hard and after being with the organisation for 4 years, I left my paid employment and ventured out on my own to provide BAS and

Bookkeeping services. I was qualified and certified. The world was my oyster and I was in control of my own destiny.

I look back now reflecting on all that study effort, hard dedicated work and discrimination experienced within the building industry and wonder whether it was all worth it in the end. I could have had such an easier time if I had remained working in training and development. As I reflect on it now I believe that possibly the universe was telling me to FINALLY stand up for myself and recognise those skills I had and that I didn't need a male supervisor telling me I was not accepted in the workplace because I wanted to be a mother as well. I am grateful now that I had the courage to open my own business and leave paid employment. I also proved to myself how good my skills actually are and how confident and talented I truly am.

Please note that changing jobs is not easy option, in fact it's the harder path at times. Starting over each time brings new challenges as well as opportunities and the need to prove yourself in the workplace with new people and fit into another workplace environment is exhausting at times. However my resilience and ability to adapt to new environments has been at the core of my success in moving from workplace to workplace. The courage to change and push myself outside my comfort zone started early in life. It helped me nurture that entrepreneurial nature within me and that desire to empower others. The new connections with new people helped me to see my world differently, and helped me reach a greater understanding of the different types of people that make up our unique world and who I was within it. What I did learn was that my way of thinking in this world was definitely influenced by my family, how I was raised and my culture. In the end my diversity is what makes me special and trying to dull down my uniqueness is not necessary. People just need to accept me as I am, including myself.

Despite the struggles of not achieving a second pregnancy through IVF, I surged ahead and created the work-life balance I wanted for my family. I have successfully operated my own bookkeeping practice for the past 12 years and have assisted over 25 small businesses in Adelaide with their bookkeeping needs. I feel very grateful for this opportunity in my work life. This constant change and adaptation from job to job helped me in my own business in the end as adapting to new workplaces and new procedures had become second nature by that stage of my life.

The dedication required to run a small business has honestly been difficult at times, juggling my family's needs and client deadlines. However the flexibility of being able to attend to your only child's needs and then co-ordinating your work time around schooling and sporting requirements has been the best decision I ever made in my life.

Most importantly I now have the choice to choose who I work with and can be my true, authentic ethnic self.

Surprisingly I have not received any discrimination since opening my own business and working with many small businesses, even though most of these small businesses are managed by men. If I work with clients that do not treat their staff well, they are usually not clients I align to and I terminate their contract. I simply do not support those practices personally.

Ironically, despite all that effort and discrimination, I still feel a pull to work in the building industry. It is like some things are still unresolved and need to be revisited. I am pleased to have the opportunity this year to work back in the building industry again. I am hoping that this time my passion for working within this industry will be rewarded. My circumstances have changed; I am no longer pregnant or juggling IVF while being a mother to a toddler.

I feel all women in all work environments need to work on empowering each other and not work against each other. It is hard enough working in industries where you are the minority and there are unequal pay levels and opportunities in the workplace. We have enough competition around us and we should be united together. If not, there will never be an improvement in the workplace for all women moving forward, especially for the next generation of women to come. United we can all make a difference in the world.

For all the Giussa and ethnic women out there that are currently feeling stuck in their careers and work life balance: you can change. Feel the fear and do it anyway. That's what I did and in the end everything is a learning experience whether the change works out or not. Be brave and teach your kids to do the same in life.

The full transformation to being my authentic self in all aspects of my life is currently a work in progress. Writing this book has been in some ways the final push to really be my true unapologetic, authentic self, free of all guilt and concerns of judgement by others.

Most importantly I have learned that even if no one else in the world around you celebrates you or acknowledges your hard work, learn to celebrate and encourage yourself. It is not really up to other people to keep you going, it's up to you from the inside.

Part Two

Our Italian Traditions

John's parents were migrants that travelled by boat for one month to Australia, with their own families as young adults. My mother-in-law arrived as a young child with her siblings and parents. My father-in-law arrived with his brothers as a young 17-year-old. His parents arrived later to join some of their children in Adelaide once they were settled. Both parents were from a region in Naples called Molinara. The Molinarese community in Adelaide is quite large as the town was devastated by an earthquake which resulted in many migrating to Adelaide to resettle. It was like another version of their town in the eastern suburbs of Adelaide. They followed many of the Italian cultures that were practised in their village. I have been part of many of these traditions including sauce making day, sausage making, pizza making, wine making and helping at the Molinara club events. My father-in-law was the president of the club during a time when John was young. Both parents have contributed heavily and volunteered their time within the club and the community their entire lives, along with their children.

The Molinara club was a place we spent a lot of time as a family, participating in cultural events and functions with other families and friends that John grew up with. It was such a wonderful time, further experiencing the Italian part of my heritage with my in-laws and their extended family. I felt so included by others and I learnt a lot about the bond this community had with each other, in addition to their dedication to maintaining their heritage for future generations.

My husband has been fortunate to have the influence of his grandmother who lived to 109 years of age! She lived 6 months of the year on a rotating roster with John's parents and other uncles. Her influence in the family was very visible. She was much loved and she showed much love to her family: especially the grandchildren. An article was written about her in the newspaper when she reached 109 and they asked her what the key to living a long life was. Her answer was simple: to enjoy life and have everything in moderation and to practice and have faith. She also personally told her grandson John, that another key to living a good life was to surround yourself with good people and speak your mind. This advice is something that he always tries to implement in his own life.

I feel that John was more fortunate than me with having such an extended family. He had benefited from being surrounded by not only very extended family but also his grandparents. For a long time he experienced the love and kindness that only grandparents can give to their grandchildren, along with their wisdom and knowledge. John's perspective on tradition and heritage is again different from mine as my Italian upbringing did not include any grandparents or uncles, aunties and cousins. My parents came here on their own so we only had my mother's uncle's family, and we were grateful to become part of the extended family on my great auntie's side.

My parents were also part of an Italian club called the Abruzzi club, in the western suburbs of Adelaide. This was aligned to my dad's region in Italy. My parents also participated and volunteered their time during the start up of the club when we were growing up and dad regularly played bocce there with the other men from his region. I was part of the initial youth group when the club first started with my sisters and was the youth group's president a few years later in my 20's helping to lead the group, co-ordinate functions with other Italian youths and raise funds for the club's facilities to involve more youth.

This aspect of volunteering as children and youth within our cultural communities helped us develop our own links to our heritage along with our parents. In this way we developed our individual ties and connections to our regions in Italy. It was a great family activity and one the parents were proud we were part of. Most families knew each other and they felt their kids were safe running around the halls enjoying themselves with the other children. We were the next generation of their ethnic culture and I feel were fortunate to have these ethnic clubs during our era so that we could meet others that understood our background and our values without explaining it.

My friends and I often discuss our heritage and what it really means. We talk about why we want to carry on the traditions that are now a lot of hard work within our present busy lives, and why our kids all want to come with us to look and help. The cultural, rustic food aspect is definitely something that strongly links us to our heritage. However it is also something more powerful and intrinsic than simply the preparation of food, making the sauce or sausage or picking the grapes from the vine. It is actually the internal feeling of where you belong, why you are the way you are and that your parents taught you well. Standing next to another individual who is your parent or family member working on a mutually beneficial task sometimes doesn't even need words or conversation. Sometimes you just got a nod from your dad that you were on the right path and those tomato pieces you were shoving in the recycled bottle was correctly done and you were doing a good job. This is where we got our acknowledgement from our parents that we were doing a good job in the sauce making process and really it was also a nod that we were doing ok in our life as well. They were proud of us as their children and seeing us help them make this type of food together made them more proud of us and we could feel that. That's the bit the children of first-generation Italian immigrants we want to feel again and keep feeling and pass on to our kids to feel. That's called family love: the Italian way. Doing Italian things together and being with each other and supporting each other together as one family unit.

Italian parents didn't overly compliment their kids and they didn't usually tell you how good you were to boost your self-esteem or self-worth. It was more of a tough love approach with many ethnic parents. I know that my dad was not really capable of telling me that he loved me, not in the way I verbalise it to my child on a daily basis (and sometimes several times a day). I knew both my parents loved me and they were proud of me, but my mum was better at verbalising it. My dad didn't know how to say those words easily. He didn't know how to express himself like that, he wasn't capable of it, but he could give me the nod when we did tasks together and I felt it that way.

"Ok dad? Like this?"

"Si Claudia."

The Old Italy, the New Italy and the Australian-Italians

When people that immigrated to Australia in the 1950's and 60's finally go back to their village in their home town they are often shocked by how much their fellow Italian friends and villagers have changed. In particular, that they are no longer as traditional as they once were. They would often remark to their friends that they are way too modern - especially their children - and that God forbid no one really gets married in Italy, they just live together. It is often said that the Italians in Australia are more Italian than those in Italy. One reason for this was that when they migrated, in their minds time simply stopped once they arrived in Australia. Despite embracing their new culture, in order for them to feel confident and brave many held on to their traditions. They then enforced those restrictions and traditions on to their first-generation children. They were not impressed that their fellow Italians who stayed within their village had modernised and changed their approach. They were grateful they had kept their traditions alive in Australia. However this created another level of what being Italians in Australia really represented. When they returned to Italy they didn't feel like the other Italians and when they arrived back home to Australia they were not quite fully Australian (nor did they want to be). This essentially created a sub-culture in Australia: it was the Italian-Australian culture. We were the children born into that new sub-culture with ethnic old traditional rules that the children in Italy were not adhering to and again a different set of rules to the real Aussie born kids.

We are the product of this merged culture and we are again redefining it for our children.

The sad thing is that our immigrant parents are often still yearning for that village they were born in and those times again. I know that as my father developed early-onset dementia he talked about those times with such fond memories despite leaving his village over 60 years ago.

He still had one foot stuck in that era and the other in Australia. He never was able to speak English fluently and yet he no longer belonged in Italy. His Italian language skills had also suffered as he spoke many sentences, half in Italian and half English sounding Italian words. The funny thing is that we understood him completely and so did many other Australian-Italians. The cousins left in Italy however didn't and would struggle to understand their uncle over the phone. Not only was there a sub-culture but there was also the development of a new sub-language unique to Australian-Italians that was alive and well.

It's funny how the purpose of all of the cultural activities I participated in as a child in both the Italian and French languages was to ensure that I could actually in fact speak and write well in both languages. Well, I'm embarrassed to say that compared to my mother and three other sisters, my language skills are not that great. My mother worked at her hospital role in administration, then once we were in high school, she studied to become a medical interpreter and was also called upon at times to help Italian patients with their medical appointments. My older sister specialised and became a French and Italian language teacher, while both my other sisters went overseas and worked in areas that enabled them to use their French language skills on a regular basis. Then there was me. I averaged 'C' grades in both languages at school because I was especially lazy, never really studied that hard in year 10 and mostly tried to 'wing it'. What a wasted opportunity. I do actually have a good level of understanding of both languages and can follow most conversations, including the Italian dialect of Naples and Abruzzo, however, due to a lack of confidence I have become quite shy at speaking both languages, especially Italian.

When I met John, his family automatically assumed I was fluent at speaking Italian as my mother and sisters were good at it and I could clearly understand the conversation around the dinner table. I did try hard; however, I would resort to doing exactly what my dad would do and 'Australianise' the words I didn't know. This caused so much laughter, especially from the overseas visitors who would simply look at me confused at the words I would jumble together to try to get my point across. Then they would giggle and correct me.

Out of all my sisters, I needed that Italian language skill the most, as I was the only one that married into another Italian family and was surrounded by the language and activities that went along with it.

John often tells a story that when he started to come over more regularly to my house for dinner, he couldn't follow the dinner conversation at times. That was because we spoke French, Italian and English to our parents: sometimes we spoke all three in the same sentence. I would be the one child that did it the most as I would substitute words that I didn't know across all three languages. My dad worked in Belgium so he also knew conversational French. I would generally start off in Italian, and then add in some French, and if I didn't know the rest of the words, I would finish off in English with a slight accent to make it sound Italian. John would turn to me and say: "I got five out of ten words. What else did you say?" He would jokingly ask if I was sure my family was from an Italian background because we sounded like we were speaking a completely different language. I would respond: "Well at least I know three languages: how many have you got up your sleeve?"

I developed a bit of a funny reputation because of my language skills. When older relatives asked if I spoke Italian, I would respond with "un Pochettino." I thought that translated to: "a little, or, a tiny bit." They then understood that I could understand enough to get by, but I wasn't really fluent. Well, little did I know that actual word doesn't exist and again I had simply Australianised it! The correct phrase is "un po" (a little bit), or "solo un pochino" (just a tiny bit). I was adding "tino" as it rhymes with tiny, and then saying it with an Italian accent. Most of our Italian relatives and others in Adelaide knew what I meant. Nobody ever corrected me. Well, along come John's cousins from Switzerland (whom I love dearly) visiting us in Adelaide. When I responded to their question of whether I spoke Italian with "un Pochettino", they laughed so hard! From that point on they told everyone how funny I was, commenting that: "Only in Australia that would happen… and only Claudia."

From embarrassment comes laugher and connection. My nickname is now 'Pochettino' and I am introduced to all their overseas friends and relatives by this name. I actually love it. It would only happen to a Giussa!

I am not the only person in Adelaide or Australia that finds it hard with the Italian language. Many of us simply learnt it from our parents in the home and most of the time that was their dialect - not the proper, formal Italian. I am envious of those from my generation that have in fact learned to speak it well: my husband is one of them. It is a very useful skill and handy to have up your sleeve. When we travelled to Italy for our honeymoon, he was confident enough for the both of us to be able to travel easily around Italy. We would walk around the local village in both our parents' towns; John conversing fluently with the locals like he had lived there all his life! We subsequently felt right at home and part of the culture. Unfortunately, it has been harder for my son Marcus to learn the language and be confident in speaking it. His Italian studies in high school have only taught him so much. This is why our generation was so fortunate: we were immersed in the richness of the Italian language at home, regularly hearing it spoken by our parents. Even if we responded back to them in English, that immersion in the language is one of the things that helps us to remain connected to our culture, and makes us proud Italians born in Australia. Recently, Marcus asked that we speak more Italian at home to him so that he can get better at talking in the language. My response was "you had better learn from your dad; he is better than me. I will only teach you words that probably don't even exist in the Italian language – don't forget why my nickname is Pochettino."

Ethnic Children Are Loved Deeply

I can say that I am loved despite every frustrating road block and every argument I had with my parents, especially my dad. I was born from love and everything my parents and family did for me was out of love. I know this from my core. This deep love gave me confidence to love others and to express myself to the world around me. Even though it never felt like that and it just felt like they were constantly trying to control my life and make me into someone they wanted me to be and to follow their rules, never once did I feel like I was not loved.

I think that is why we ethnics are expressive individuals. We are confident in expressing our love and giving hugs and kisses on the cheeks, even to strangers. We have love and passion running through our veins. We are a group that not only express our love through words but also through the physical aspect of touch and hugs that we give to our family and friends that reinforce our love. This simple aspect I feel is what makes us Australian-Italians unique.

We are great at loving all things and being loud and laughing loudly. We interrupt each other's stories and add our own bit, with more laughing and slapping each other: physically showing that we are enjoying their company and presence.

We are too loud and over the top according to my Australian-Scottish brother-in-law who barely copes with our noise level at an immediate family cake and coffee birthday gathering for the family kids' parties. That's about 40 people invited to our house for the immediate family when I host my side of the family birthdays. We are all ok with his disappearing act into some quiet bedroom to take refuge away from the noisy and loud ethnics and then usually resurfacing when the cake is being cut. It must be confronting if you have not grown up with it. Apparently the pitch of our voices just gets really high whenever we are together. It's like we are at the soccer cheering for Adelaide United but we are actually in a house having cake and coffee for a birthday.

I have tried to determine if we are really that loud and over the top with the hugging and kissing. This is normal for us; this is how we were brought up and the family gatherings we are used to. His usual response is that "nothing your family do is at a normal talking level; it is all screaming like you're having an argument and you're all talking and laughing over each other and interrupting … too much commotion and noise for me and my head is usually spinning in the end! My childhood was nothing like that in Australia. We all sat calmly and quietly around the table each taking turns with our conversation, never interrupting each other and celebrating at a normal tone."

Yes, I suppose we are all different in our family environment. But bloody hell - we ethnics sure know that we are connecting, having a good time and that we are loved and loving life! I'll take my family any day, thanks! Loud, laughing and connecting with each other. Living life at full volume for me, please.

Calm conversation at a normal tone never happened at my house and never in conversations with my father. I felt that I had to be louder than him just to be heard and understood. This never really worked, nor was it an effective strategy of actually getting my own way. I didn't care in the moment; I was determined to be just as stubborn as him when I needed to be.

I would start with: "Oh why, why, why, is it NO, NO, NO, as your first answer every time? You don't even know any details yet!"

My husband constantly tells me to lower my voice when I am discussing something with him that is emotional or if I am very excited. "Sorry honey that's the way I am. I am not arguing with you, just showing the passion and intensity of something that I am feeling." This is also a residual effect of growing up in my family unfortunately. Speak louder and you feel like you're being heard.

My argumentative family discussions growing up were always emotional and intense as I felt that I was never really understood. I couldn't speak Italian very well and my dad couldn't speak English very well. As a result I felt we couldn't get the right words out to have those sensitive conversations, especially when I was a teenager and being told that I was not allowed to do anything that my friends were doing freely.

My mother's English was at a higher level as she worked in an office and could read and write very well. This meant I would always run to my mum for a discussion on whether I could do this or that and she was fully aware of her daughter's movements. If required she would discuss my various requests with my father in Italian.

Sometimes if the event was important to me and the answer was "no" I would lose my temper and start debating his reasoning with him, directly at full speed and usually at a high pitch. My dad couldn't understand my argumentative nature and why I would dare to question his decisions in this manner. In his mind our parent's generation were never allowed to argue with their parents and so they felt that our generation shouldn't be allowed to discuss it with them or even think about arguing with them: let alone at full speed in screaming English. My older sister worked it out better than I did. She would plant a seed about something weeks in advance during normal conversation, then come back to it a few days later and warm him up about it and *bang* he would come around and allow it. She was good at the Italian language and could converse very well.

OMG, do I need to strategic plan just to go out and do my own thing? Too much work and effort!

The cultural rules and the inability to communicate well unfortunately caused many arguments in my world and I would get quite sad about it. They loved us deeply but in terms of verbally communicating this, it was very hard for them to express the right words sometimes in either language. But they did love us and just wanted to keep us safe and we knew that, despite us not agreeing with their decisions.

My mum and I could communicate very well. Our conversations were more in line with discussing pros and cons of the request and at least I felt that my voice was heard and I was understood. However, her hands were tied in many ways as my dad would overrule some of her decisions that she thought were reasonable: just because he was the head of the family. My mum would remind me that my dad grew up in a small village in Abbruzzo, Italy, he was not educated past grade 5 primary school level and then was sent to work to help provide for the family. She would tell me, "His ability to verbally reason with you is not at the skill level that you have developed with your schooling and you need to consider that when you're discussing things of a sensitive nature with him. Furthermore discussing things with him in anger will just shut him down as he will perceive it to be disrespectful and the result will be a NO even if it was a feasible request to start with." I felt like I could never win. I was stuck in the middle. Many of my ethnic friends also experienced this within their homes and communication skills were not their parents' forte either.

In the end as I got older I would tell my parents very little regarding my plans and goals. The less they knew, the less likely they could have any impact on them. I learned to live in two worlds and the hiding of things or being secretive became my way for some things. It was not my preference but it enabled me to cope better both with the family rules and living in the external world. So this ended up being a strategy most of my life and crossed over to the workplace.

At times this was exhausting trying to juggle all the different people I was meant to be in all the different areas of my life.

Our parents - like many other Italian immigrants - left their birth land for a better world for us children. They were brave to go and live in a foreign country with no direct family support. They had to learn a foreign language and their children were often more educated than them and had more work opportunities. They sacrificed their own development and security for the benefit of a better life. They arrived and their first focus was to work and earn a living to support their family and settle and buy their home. They didn't attend schooling and many had gone to work early in Italy to help their poor parents support the family. In fact my dad often sent money back to his parents to help them from Belgium and Australia. The family commitment and support was always there despite the distance. I know all immigrants are hard workers and my mum and dad sacrificed a lot and worked many hours to support us. My parents were exhausted by the time the weekend came around and simply wanted to enjoy their home, garden and have a beautiful meal with their family.

Reflecting back on their start in the Australian community they did an excellent job in assimilating and building a community around them. Try to add an argumentative female teenager on top of that screaming at them "why, why, why, not" and probably not even understanding what she was saying in the first place … I would have said no to everything as well!

Now the shoe is on the other foot and my own argumentative male teenage child is asking "why, why, why, not!" Sometimes I respond with: "Because I say so", and "it's a NO because this is my house and you are asking disrespectfully and I don't care if you don't like it … suck it up child, I am in charge." Or sometimes I am saying "Marcus my child, please be respectful of my decision and your tone and I don't want to hear the arguments or have this discussion anymore."

Oh my God I am turning into my dad!

The difference is that I can out argue my child and use big words and develop and discuss counter arguments to deflect his responses. The reality was my dad had no chance with his feisty, stubborn strong daughter. Oh, maybe I should have been a bit kinder to him in retrospect; he was just protecting one of his girls.

Ethnic Respect

This was the golden unwritten rule growing up in an Italian-Australian household. This word growing up was the essence of what you were judged by.

How you displayed your emotions, your physical stance, what you said, how you spoke, the words you used to express yourself, how you communicated with your family, how you displayed love to your family and even if you kissed and greeted everyone when you were being visited or when visiting others. This and more all forms part of what it means to show respect.

Showing respect did not only involve your immediate family or relatives, it was the entire world around you. Why? The reason why was that your actions were a reflection of your entire family. Your attitude and how you displayed respect was the test of whether you were brought up correctly by your parents. Furthermore whether your parents taught you well based on how they were brought up by their parents. The test is actually a generational one.

It sounds extreme? Surely not the entire world? Well close enough, everyone who is from an ethnic background: in Australia that is at least a third of our population.

There is no rule book that actually explains how to do this well, or what the criteria are that fall under this banner called respect. Nothing is ever explained or taught in a methodical manner. It is assumed it is known the instant you are born.

You are never taught respect explicitly. Rather you are taught via being reprimanded when you are not doing something correctly. The word *respect* was used for everything from leaving the empty toilet roll in the bathroom to not giving a distant relative kisses on the cheek the moment you saw them.

Growing up I heard phrases like:

- Did you ask me permission to do that – where is your respect for my authority?
- Don't act like that – that is not very respectful.
- That's no way to show me respect.
- Your opinion is not showing respect towards me as the head of the family.
- You're not eating the food I prepared – show some respect.

Ethnic Values

Essentially: We do all the right things in life for our family.

- We have respect and we speak to each other respectfully.
- We listen to our parents and their opinions.
- We care about our family and make time for them and their personal needs.
- We respect our elders.
- We celebrate together as a family and community.
- We have children and we expand our family unit.
- We work hard at our jobs or in school.
- We save our money and be resourceful.
- We are honest and kind to others.
- We do not take people for granted.
- We treat others how we like to be treated.
- We have hope and faith in life.

These values are not foreign concepts to us in Australia and other cultures and they are amazing values to adhere to in life. The Italian people come from a wonderful culture that shouts out loud love, passion, hard work, family, connection and food. We Australian-Italians try to live these values every day and feel the emotion in our body and soul.

My parents instilled these values in our family and they are very noble and empowering standards to adhere to. Our parents and their parents before them were hardworking, honest, humble and respectful individuals and this is what our family represents to the world at large.

All they wanted from us as their children was to adhere to these values and celebrate their family and culture together. Reflecting on those statements, they are in fact the same values we want for our children now. When you didn't achieve these values you were then subjected to what we call "Ethnic Guilt". A passive aggressive tactic our parents used to make us feel bad so we would adhere to their rules.

Behaving well as ethnic children came from our discomfort and the feeling of guilt as we became so highly in tune with our parents needs that at times even when they didn't show us the anger or say they were disappointed with us we got the message – we knew we were letting them down before we even came face to face with them.

We are more sensitive in conducting our relationships with our children and we are not trying to destroy their self-esteem when they have failed at something or disappointed us with their behaviour. We want our children to have good values but also know when it is the right time to stand up for themselves and not be bullied by anyone.

I feel the difference with our own children is in our delivery and our kinder and less judgemental approach in teaching them the values. We don't simply state "you must respect me." Instead we have a conversation about the importance of respecting others' opinions and talking to others in a polite way. We use examples of good behaviour and bad behaviour to get our message across. We try not to simply give them the ethnic look of disappointment or physical punishment when they have not met our expectations.

Don't get me wrong, I wish the ethnic "don't you dare misbehave" look worked on my child every time. He would be like: "What mum? I didn't say anything! "Or "What? I haven't done anything wrong.. geez!"

The upside of this confidence of our children to converse and discuss their issues with us as parents will hopefully ensure that my child can be honest with me about his feelings and emotions. I hope that he will not be like me and simply not say anything for fear of judgement and being reprimanded unfairly. I want my child to know that his opinion counts; for him to feel that he can contribute to the discussion and not simply get dismissed due to age or gender. However this doesn't mean that his opinion will be validated on every occasion. We still need to be parents and make the final safe and best choices for them while they are young.

Our parents and their parents grew up in different times. Many endured the difficulties of the war and famine as children and then they immigrated across the other side of the world without knowing the language. They endured harder times compared to us born in Australia.

We often felt the weight of our parents' immigrant dreams on our shoulders and we needed to achieve and not make any mistakes in life. Maybe it was a validation for them and their decision to be courageous, and that our success was confirmation that it was all worth the pain and heartache they endured. Mental health was not a word that existed when we grew up and their focus was making their children more resilient through tough love and strictness and adherence to their cultural values, not their child's unique talents or personality.

As adults in this current era, we want to ensure that our children do not feel the same burdens on their shoulders that we had growing up. We want them to have the opportunity to simply be children and to live life without the pressure of feeling guilty. We want our children to be resilient yet not at the expense of their self-worth or to feel that failure in life is not an option.

Keeping the Ethnic Traditions

My mother worked full-time in medical records in a hospital. Because of this I felt that she didn't align her self-esteem only to her place in the kitchen; she didn't see it as her only domain in life and tried to achieve a work-life balance with her family. My mother's outlook was far more modern than she realised at the time. My mum would still make traditional foods with my dad helping her at times, yet she did this out of her own pleasure of being in the kitchen and making her favourite dishes such as gnocchi, braciola and fermented and pickled vegetables.

Her sisters in Belgium were even more progressive and changed more rapidly in comparison to my mother. In some ways they felt that some of the traditions that my mother maintained were out of date compared to them still living in Europe. They certainly didn't make homemade sauce or even homemade pasta or pizza at home, despite also marrying immigrant Italians in Belgium. That was their mother's era, yet my mother carried on those traditions in Australia when she migrated here with my father. My father loved being immersed in these traditions and felt very much aligned to other migrants. He rejoiced at the thought of being able to maintain the traditions he was brought up with.

Along with their sheer courage and bravery came the need to keep their traditions alive. They knew in their hearts that although the land they were going to would provide more opportunity, leaving their traditions and families filled them with sadness. They were simply trying to hold on to every tradition they knew so they would be able to cope in this new world. It was their control mechanism and the structure of the traditions gave them a feeling they had a safety net. As young ethnic children we were given all these traditions to follow and it gave our lives structure also.

My child has grown up with us being very social and constantly being surrounded with our families and friends. Despite our busyness we are always connecting and like our parents we often connect through food and entertaining people with food. Ethnic tradition, especially in the Italian community, is built around the concept of food and eating as a family at the table together.

Doing the Ethnic Visits

We ethnics never turn up to anyone's house without a small gift. This gift is to thank them for the invitation to their home. Gift examples are the traditional Panettone (especially at Christmas), wine, chocolates, or the specialty Italian cakes. They open the door, say hello, hugs and kisses and then you shove the gift in their hands with their response usually being: "Oh you didn't have to bring anything! This is too much! Thank you, you are very kind." This is not usually said a normal pitch voice … even the "hiiii" is at alto pitch.

We know that even a pop in visit (except for your parents-in-laws and sibling's houses, where you get things to take home), you never go empty handed. We just can't help ourselves. Even though we know it is not really expected, we still adhere to it.

This tradition was never that grand back in my parents' generation. The gift was from their backyard produce or made in the kitchen. For my dad it was some of his home-grown peaches or lemons from his trees or my mum's homemade pizzas or biscuits. Their gift was priceless and derived from their unique skills, heart and soul. Not a purchased gift from the supermarket a few hours before the visit is to take place.

Still to this day it is not uncommon for us to return from our parents' home with bags of fruit, bread, cakes or even extra spinach my mum bought from the market for us girls because we need some extra iron infused veggies for our busy lives.

The pop in visit concept has changed in comparison to our parents' generations. Back then you simply turned up at their front door and rang the doorbell and called out: "Compare Mario here…Permesso." The entire family would come to the door and see who came over. Everyone gathered together in the kitchen or dining room for the entire visit and you interacted with them or helped your mum prepare the coffee and nibbles. It wasn't a big showy event but you did always get the good set of coffee cups and glasses out for these types of visits. Coffee was also served several times before they actually left. Your parents would say: "Come on Compare and Comare, stay for another drink of Strega or espresso." Now we all call ahead of time even if you are at the top of their street ringing to check whether you should stop and get out of the car. Now most of our visits to each other's homes are pre-scheduled and planned in advance. Many in the younger generation prefer cafes and restaurants for catch up venues as no one wants to cook and clean up for anyone else anymore.

However, recently I have found that our kids now want to align back to our generation and stay home when we have friends over for our rustic food feasts and catch ups. They love the food, the banter, the conversations and heartfelt connections that our gatherings create. They want their toes in both worlds, so to speak. A great home cooked meal prepared traditional style surrounded by family and friends, then at about 11pm all happily filled with free food and alcohol, they UBER off to meet their friends at the clubs until all hours of the night. As they depart we thank them for their presence and tell them not to worry about helping with the clean up and to enjoy their young life. "Oh great" they say, "we will." We were not expecting them to offer to clean up in any event.

We would never have been that brazen with our parents! In fact, I think we would have been questioned by our parents with: "Where do you think you're going now at his hour of the night? Go help your mother in the kitchen please, then off to bed."

Despite our busy lives, this tradition of gift giving and visiting still stands as a great ethnic tradition we love to maintain and even our non-ethnic Australian friends who we visit love it as well.

Christmas Day

All Italians love Christmas. We usually go all out and buy food to celebrate and cook for days preparing for the one day event. The problem is that it is only one day and you have to accommodate which side of the family gets the day time slot for Christmas day lunch - it is like the gold wrapper in the movie *Charlie and the Chocolate Factory!*

Conversation leading up to Christmas within our friendship group is usually about which side of the family got Christmas day lunch. Who was allocated to the night before or the night time Christmas day slot? Or did the Christmas calendar fall with your parents' side or the in-laws? Is it the on year or the off year? "Oh this year is my mum's turn and she is so happy that she gets to have the lunch time spot and so excited to be serving and eating her famous lasagne and eating the zeppolis."

Essentially we Italians have such simple pleasures and it's really all about the food and getting that prized lunch time slot with your family. Then you spend the rest of the day fully carb-bloated, visiting the other side or the relatives and complaining that you ate too much food.

Italians and Money

Money is the essence of all discussions within the Italian community. How much it cost, what you paid for this or that, what properties you have, how much rent you get, where you work, what do you make, how much was your car, how much did the trip cost, how many kids you have and how expensive they are, what do you pay for school fees, how's business going, you making a million dollars yet?

The list is endless and no money topic is usually off limits, especially within your immediate family. It sounds very offensive and most people answer and exaggerate and embellish. It's the Italian way and we are used to those conversations, as they were the types of discussions at the dinner table and relatives' houses growing up. The disadvantage of this casual money discussion is that everything is also measured in dollar value. People's success is therefore determined by dollar value rather than the happiness in their hearts and faces.

Our effective use of time is at times also measured in whether this will add value in terms of monetary gain rather than feeding our passion and willingness to simply help others for no gain. I personally came across some negative comments in starting my small business Shining Light and writing my book. Some comments were simply about not wasting my time on such ventures unless there would be a significant monetary gain for all that time I devoted to these projects. These comments usually came from other ethnic males and females from my generation and I believe actually highlights more about their values regarding money rather than mine. I would simply respond by saying some things in life are not about money but about achieving personal dreams and living life with a purpose.

Our parents came with nothing and they were happy with what possessions they were able to afford and they valued money in a different way to us. Sometimes I feel our generation needs to be reminded of this.

Let's be mindful of money influences and conversations in our own world and around our children. We sometimes spend too much time worrying about money and working too hard for it most of our lives. It is also important to realise that it is not the ultimate key to success and definitely will not feed our souls or hearts. I definitely do not want my child to think of money as the be all and end all of life's success and worth.

Part Three

Changing the Narrative for the Next Generation: Hopes for My Child

I asked my son: "What nationality do you say you are?"

"Australian-Italian" was his response. "I am definitely Italian because you and dad are Italian."

I was surprised with this quick response regarding being Italian. I then advised him that dad and I were actually born in Australia so that makes us technically fully Australian from an Italian heritage. You are therefore technically second generation Australian. He then said, "yes, I understand that mum, but I'm still Italian. It's my heritage I am referring to and besides there is more to someone's nationality than their place of birth."

So, there you go: that's what my 16-year-old son has decided all on his own. I feel he is more ethnic than I was at his age!

What Our Children Want From Us as Ethnic Raised Parents

There are many stories of ethnic Australian-born children from my era receiving very direct discrimination at school. We were ethnics, we ate ethnic food and we often felt and were treated as being different. Growing up we all tried to assimilate and not have any attention directed our way. We cringed every time we were called names. Even though I had friends, they were all the same as me: ethnic Australian with similar parents like myself and that really meant no play dates at each other's houses. I always felt that my vocabulary in both French and Italian that I was speaking from an early age was not something to be proud of, especially if my English spelling words were not correct.

In primary school we all wanted to have vegemite sandwiches in our lunch box, not stinky salami. I wanted to have cheese Twisties and buttered Bush Biscuits from the tuck shop for recess, not the home grown fruit from our backyard tree and fennel taralli my mum made. I wanted to be invited to birthday parties, play pin the tail on the donkey, eat fairy bread and go home with a lolly bag. I also wanted to be allowed to have a similar birthday party of my own with my friends.

When people asked me growing up what nationality I was I would answer "I was born in Australia, why?" I knew I felt different from other Anglo-Australians, but I didn't want to be treated differently. I wanted to blend in so that I received the same school and work opportunities as the others. So I would often be offended by them asking. "Are you trying to single me out now?" I would often think.

I have heard many racist stories and know that some individuals had to overcome many difficult scenarios both at home and at school. I was more fortunate in this area that despite feeling the discrimination surround me many times, I also attended a Catholic primary and high school where at least 50% of the girls that attended the school were from ethnic immigrant families like me. Despite mixing with all individuals in my class the girls who I aligned myself with were mainly people that had a similar home life to me. At school they preached about being kind and loving to all people in this world and our nun principal was very multicultural orientated.

The next generation of children have not experienced the level of racism we endured as children and living with strict ethnic parents in the 1980's. Despite this, a 2020 study found millennials are the most stressed generation on record.

So what changed now for our children's generation? I believe that as Australians we have in some way finally truly embraced the multicultural environment and we all work at not being racist and accepting each other's uniqueness. Our children are very good in this area and I feel that their generation is less judgemental and more accepting of the diversity of our culture.

We accepted the culture of our parents, and on some occasions it was forced upon us. Often we cringed and moved away from its diversity and tried to tone it down. Our children accept that everyone in Australia is from somewhere and they are now looking for a way to align themselves to some cultural group and connect to something through us, their parents. They are not looking at toning it down, they want it celebrated out loud and they want to connect to the things they like about their parents' culture.

That is also the key in this scenario. What they want from the culture is not the entire cultural package. Our children actually want to feel diverse; they want to have a point of difference in this big vast technology driven world of ours.

Our children live in a world immersed in technology and despite being able to connect with people all over the world through technology it is in fact a VIRTUAL connection – they are not able to reach out and touch or connect in a physical sense, even with some of the people they may talk to on a daily basis over the internet.

For many children of this generation, their world is lived usually through a phone in their hands and their heart skips a beat every time the phone dings. Connection is measured by likes or comments on a page or the endless quick messages that they receive. This, I feel they are discovering, is not real connection, no matter how popular they are.

They want real moments… real food … real family moments… real connection … real love and laugh out loud moments. They want to sit around the dinner table and have real conversations.

So you are saying what - is it that simple? Our children do not want to be experiencing constant busyness of life and want to have real time with the family? Hey mate we are loving that message, let's bring it on.

Changing the Rules for Our Children's Wellbeing

"Sorry Marcus, ethnic families do not allow children to sleep over for birthday parties or any reason for that fact. You can stay out later than normal - even up to 1am - however I will pick you up and the rule is that you sleep in your own bed so that I know you are safe and sound for the rest of the night. I do not sleep well when you are away from home at someone else's house or when you are out late at night. There is always that feeling something is going to happen. You will only know that when you're a parent yourself so please respect our decision in this area. I will always wait up for you until I know that you are home safe and then I can rest my head on my pillow. This is simply what parents do."

"Mum, that's a ridiculous rule! Just because you were not allowed to growing up that doesn't mean that it is a great reason for you not to let me. You allow me to sleep over at Nonna's and my auntie's houses yet not with my friends. All my friends' parents let their children do it. I'm the only one left out!"

"My sisters and your grandparents are an extension of our family and I know they have the same values and care about you the same way we do. Are the other parents ethnic, Marcus? Other children's parents have been brought up differently and we try to follow our own family rules." This argument went on for at least 5 years, much to his annoyance.

When he turned 15, I decided that it was in fact a bit over the top and that if I could be ok with allowing him to go on camp with the school for three days, I could now allow the sleep over rule to lapse for the occasional birthday overnighter. My thoughts then propelled me to the future when he has a girlfriend and if the other rule about no sleeping at each other's houses overnight would be just as difficult to overcome. I certainly remember the anger I faced over the same rule my parents enforced on myself and the eight year wait I endured, tip toeing around until I was married. I was so strict regarding the no sleepover rule and have been reflective on whether I will be able to change my behaviour to allow him to be his own person and make his own decisions at that stage of his life. Will society and our community still feel that it's okay for his rules to be different because he is male? Will I feel at that time as his mother to give him the complete power to shape his own life? I think so, time will tell.

What Do We Want to Pass On to Our Children?

I have noted that most of my life - and especially since I became a parent - my deeper connections were often made with females who were of the same background as me, despite the age difference. They simply 'got me' with very few words. They understood my nature, my ethnic point of view, my values, my expectations and my standards of how I would raise my child. In fact I was the most open and authentic even at our first encounters as we often faced a similar journey and family life.

Some of these women were Australian-Italian and others of another ethnic background (i.e., Greek, Polish, Croation, Maltese). One Greek friend pointed out recently that it was simply the same childhood story but in a different language. We were all influenced by our immigrant parents and their own unique story. All our parents tried to instil their cultural rules and values and deeply influence us in our lives as children and sometimes into our adulthood. Our parents imparted the values that they knew as taught by their parents.

One of my reasons for writing this book was also about the regular conversations and sometimes very funny discussions I was having with other parents about raising our children and how difficult and different it was from our generation. We would always laugh about the experiences we had as children. In some cases I know full well that some of those experiences were difficult, however through humour many of us simply try to accept the journey we went through and accept the experience for what it was during that time. We accept our parents for who they were and the sacrifices they made coming to Australia for a better life. That better life was for us, their children.

My conversation was often centred on the rules girls had to adhere to and that role in life and the expectations that were unfairly placed on us based on our gender. In actual fact, males also faced different pressures and were not excluded from the ethnic rules by their parents. Both genders had pressure and experienced high expectations from our immigrant parents. We all received the guilt whenever we did something they didn't approve of and the controlling rules used to keep us in line and safe from danger.

We all note that the traditions did in fact help provide a sense of belonging to our families and the greater community. So, the question we ask ourselves as parents from this immigrant background is: what can we learn from their parenting that was valuable and defined the great things of our culture, and how can we implement them with the new generation? What are the key aspects that will still give them those feelings of belonging that we received from our parents in their current digital environment?

Thanks to digital technology we know more than any generation of parents before us about the details of our children's lives. Parenting in the digital age means that we have access to a greater amount of information about our children's lives beyond what they elect to share with us. As parents of this new generation we should acknowledge that it is now possible to know too much about our kids. Sometimes we can read their conversation with their friends, know what they search online and even track their physical location. The biggest difference between our generation and our kids is that our parents simply had no way of knowing what we were up to, when we went home, how we spoke to our friends, or even where we were. And they probably slept better for it.

So, at this point you're thinking: we were not like today's teenagers, with their phones attached to their bodies and their fear of missing out so they are constantly checking on the beeps on their phones. We were never like that! I agree with most parents' opinions that the smart phones are turning our children into stunted screen zombies and technology has changed how we live. Thanks to digital technology our teenage children conduct their social lives on multiple tech levels.

At the end of the day our children are connecting with their friends through the technology that is currently available to them. They are simply children who are obsessed with their friends. Decades ago we wanted to connect with our peers just as desperately as our kids now want to connect with theirs.

I clearly remember sitting on the hallway table with the family phone pressed to the side of my head for hours on end. My dad would interrupt me and advise me that five minutes on the phone was sufficient talking to my friends. I would respond that we were in fact talking about home work! *Laugh out loud*! Without a doubt he would return five minutes later and advise me that talking on the phone with the corridor light on was not necessary and a waste of electricity. He would promptly switch off the light and I was left talking in the dark. That still didn't deter me - I could talk underwater if I needed to - and the darkness had no effect on interrupting the flow of conversation and connection I had with my girlfriend. I spent hours talking on the phone, sitting on the hallway telephone seat in the dark, laughing out loud with my girlfriends. In my 20's my mum finally purchased a telephone extension lead and I could grab the phone and sit in my room next to the corridor and talk in private in my bedroom with the light on.

It is normal for children to deal with painful feelings by handing their unwanted emotions off to their parents. The digital world affects our children's interpersonal lives and we probably need to learn some new strategies to help our children deal with some of the tension that comes from being plugged in all the time.

Before the days of the mobile phone, teenagers did this by casually dropping bombshells at the dinner table like we did with our parents. Some of our generation of children don't sit at the dinner table together like we did when we were growing up. I feel that based on our own background of how we were raised we simply do not have the skills to deal with this generation and their environment. Is this family dinner time without the phones being present a solution and strategy for us parents moving forward? Is regular family time together still possible in this world of never-ending commitments of out of hours sports and activities for our children? All I know is that each individual family set up is different, there just needs to be an opportunity for our children to unload their feelings somehow, just like we did.

Personally I like to be very busy as my childhood was restrictive and not filled with much adventure. As soon as I was able to co-ordinate my own life I would surround myself with lots of activities. When I became a mother, I developed this mothering activity mania. In the early days I would pack as many structured activities and plans into my day with my child. I felt that my time with my child was short and I wanted to make the most of it, especially as I only had the one child. This constant activity meant that we were often working as a family at maximum capacity and under pressure to pick up and drop off and tick the boxes.

I soon learnt that when I did not fill every waking moment with activity, the frenzy was replaced with calm, joy and spontaneous play. When my child was allowed to simply be still and play on his own with his own imagination there was a different outcome, with less rushing around and stress within the household.

Our backyard tennis on the wall and simply going outside to play and ride our bikes was one of the best times I spent as a child. My parents did not structure anything or hover over us assisting us to play and ensuring that our environment was risk assessed for safety and danger before we could start anything. Now our children are dropped off and picked up. We determine the environments they are allowed to play within, what park is better and safer, and when they should structure their friends' time after the nominated scheduled activity they are booked into most of the week and weekend.

So simply put, our children are not on any possible level operating in the same environment and they cannot be expected to just pick up on the same values we did growing up, despite us carrying those values inside us. Our children still need to express their unwanted emotions to their parents and connect with their friends and simply be allowed to do their own thing and have their own journey in their world. Despite this new environment we are within that we will probably never understand fully, they simply want a sense of belonging to us. They want to share from their hearts if they feel troubled, afraid or judged and be loved unconditionally for who they are.

Yet, as we all know, each generation has its challenges as things in the world evolve. Their world is not one that is easy either. I don't know about you, but I think this is a hard world to try and impart those family values and it is even harder when they are operating their world from within their bedrooms. Not like myself; I was out escaping into the big wide world.

Moving forward we need to reset the past; reflect on the things we want to keep from our childhood and the wisdom from our parents and adjust to the new era with a new way of connecting and belonging.

Too many ethnic parents in our era, the first-generation immigrants, were harsh on their kids. We were very impressionable. Precious and fragile at times. Some lessons learnt from our parents left long lasting impressions yet their love also helped us grow. Despite their love for us it was very much a tough love approach we received by many of our ethnic parents and surrounding families. We don't just inherit our DNA from our parents, we also absorb their best and worst behaviours. Parents should recognise that children are not possessions.

A change with how I see things and how I parent my own child is my powerful awakening in my current life.

I will enforce change within my own family, as that is the only domain I really have control over. My child will not be bound by the chains of rules that hung from my neck throughout my life, disguised under the banner of tradition. My child will have the freedom to choose which traditions he wants to carry on to his own family, just as I have the choice to carry on those that I loved. I hope that we will meet in the middle somewhere.

My approach has definitely changed as my son ages, and as I write this book reflecting on my past childhood. The one change I will definitely be making is that I now no longer try to push my agenda and control the heck out of my child. I no longer want to force my personal beliefs upon my child. I realise that in having this approach his growth may come from my discomfort.

I want to give my child the freedom to define his own version of what success is in life. Not my perceived version. I welcome him to choose his own path and to deviate from it whenever he chooses to.

I want to teach him to love and respect all individuals, especially women. I want to still impart those important Italian values I have indentified. I want him to connect his soul to our heritage and kind, like-minded people in this world. In addition to all of this, I also want to impart a sense of self belief, self-worth and the feeling that he can achieve any dream he has in this world. Above all I simply want him to be happy and laugh out loud every day.

Our Ethnic Family – Redefined by Our Generation

We extended what we defined as family in our generation. Just like our parents, we connected with like-minded people and developed friendships that formed part of our extended family group. Many of our parents' friendships were from the same region in Italy or the club associations and, on some occasions, formally connected their families through baptising and confirming each other's children.

Our generation is different in that many of us do not attend our local Italian club like our parents did. We do not only form connections with people based on our Italian heritage. Our friendship circles are more diverse and include those formed at school, workplaces, and through parents that are at the same school or sporting club as our children. Our definitions of family are broader and more inclusive: we believe that "friends are the family we choose." This also highlights the importance we place on connections within and outside our family environment and what makes our generation happy.

We recently celebrated our son's 16th birthday at an Italian food venue, with family and extended family members. The extended members included Marcus' godparents, sponsor and their families.

A total of 40 people was our classification of an immediate family celebration. These selected people we have chosen to support Marcus are not part of our immediate family tree as we wanted to extend his circle of influence and love. We know that our immediate family members will always look out for our child's needs, however these other individuals also have the same family values and unique traits that we wanted our only son to be connected to. This inclusion of others into our family unit is part of our Italian heritage and an aspect that both we and our child loves. He feels loved and special and this in turn helps nurture his emotional wellbeing in life. Outside his immediate relatives he has another five families and their family members that he is connected to in some way, and we all feel the love and connections those people bring into our small family of three people. In his eyes they are all his relatives and with pride I witnessed my only son at his birthday celebration personally greet each person individually with hugs and kisses and thanked them for coming. This is our new ethnic way for our kids and we love it and so do the kids in our family. This is what they want essentially; the family connection that wraps their souls with love and that connects them to our heritage and family ways. That, and a new iPhone upgrade every year.

Part Four

Consequences of the Ethnic Rule Book

Upon reaching the age of 50 my most wanted birthday gift was to hire a regular cleaner so that I could give myself a chance to BREATHE and not be so caught up with the constant guilt of not cleaning something in my house and returning from work to a tidy house.

What a crappy present idea at this significant age! Why wouldn't I be asking for a huge diamond rock for my finger? The wish for this ethnic chick to have someone regularly cleaning her house for her is the equivalent of getting diamonds every week!

Then I instantly felt bad at the thought of spending good, hard-earned money on someone else doing a task that I was born and raised to do for the rest of my life. I wouldn't want to be judged as lazy if I had a cleaner. I "only" had a regular full-time job and only one child to worry about. Imagine the comments! "What's wrong with her? She should be able to juggle that in her life. Our mothers did it and they regularly made homemade pasta as well and all that traditional baking every Easter and Christmas!"

The result and reality is that most of us never make time for ourselves. We always put our kids and family first. We even put the meal prepping, cleaning and decluttering and reorganising drawers of crap before we give ourselves a chance to even think about doing something different, something exciting or even better nothing at all: just plain and simple sitting on your arse on the couch or in the backyard on a chair looking up at the sky.

By the way, I have this argument with my husband at least once a year: who really cares if my linen cupboard is not neat and stacked well or evenly balanced in even piles or if the bathroom cabinet products are not correctly lined up and all in category!

Omg, whoever is worrying about that shit in life are not living their life to the fullest and must be boring individuals!

I always think about a fridge magnet we gave our mum for her birthday when she was always complaining about having to complete housework as an excuse not to have time on a Saturday to take us to the beach. The magnet said: "women who have clean houses are boring women." That magnet was on the fridge for a very long time.

My mother's house was never dirty, just a bit cluttered at times, and she had a never-ending washing and ironing basket. There were six of us in the family so that's a lot of clothes to wash every week. Sometimes my mum would ignore my dad's critical eye and remind herself that there was more to life than cooking and cleaning constantly. She never criticised another woman for her housekeeping, however, I remember her frantically cleaning the toilet and bathroom before one of our aunties came over to visit. My Aunty Connie would always ask to go to the toilet about 10 minutes into the visit. This was not because she actually needed to use it. Apparently, it was to check how clean the toilet was. The "ethnic cleaning quality control visit" we would call it. I observed that judgement and behaviour by other ethnic women regularly as a child. This constant observation resulted in reinforcing a negative behaviour in me for the rest of my life. Ethnics are really judgemental about cleaning. They may say: "Oh no, I don't judge or look at the mess, it's all okay signora." But most do and some judge and then discuss it with others, and then - even worse - measure your worth or success against it. Maybe I should give them some magnets with that saying.

I have also noted that some of us ethnic females and Giussas always apologise about the state of our houses when someone comes over and visits. I think we do this just in case their standard is not the same as our cleaning standard. We apologise for the mess prior to them stepping into the front door. This is a real lack of confidence or maybe a protective mechanism we have and it is certainly something I do subconsciously due to my upbringing.

Unfortunately, one of the unwritten ethnic rules and standards of measure for an ethnic woman is how clean her house and kids are. We are essentially guilted into making sure everything is cleaned to perfection or else we have not achieved our cultural standards.

To this day, if I host an event or dinner party at home, I usually clean the entire house from top to bottom and I am uncluttering and reorganizing for days leading up to it. You know, change things up a bit so it looks like I am on top of things in my life. I am even crawling under the middle of our bed collecting the dust balls. John always tells me: "No one is going to look under the bed Claudia.

You are going berserk cleaning like a mad woman and getting stressed and tired. Then you get all stressed about preparing the food and everyone is on high alert around you. You do this every dinner party or event!" By the way, regular yearly events are Easter, Christmas, Mother's Day, Father's Day, your family members birthdays and special occasions. That is just the family ones, then you have your friend's things as well.

Oh my god, I'm exhausted just writing this.

Then my husband asks me: "Why are you bothering hosting and having functions if you're going to get like this all the time and tire yourself out before they all arrive?" Then my mind always goes back to the ethnic quality control toilet check that Aunty Connie would perform on my mum during a simple coffee visit. My usual response is that "it is better this way so I stress less when people are here." I tell him this cleaning mania is in my ethnic veins.

I have noted that he will regularly criticise my behaviour and stand back and call my behaviour over the top or crazy.

Hey honey, how about getting that vacuum cleaner and helping me out? I am happy to direct you to the areas that I want cleaned to perfection. Oh no, he just calls me out on my craziness.

Ethnic blokes like giving their wives their opinion and cleaning directions, like they have had so much practice their entire lives. In reality they just observed their mums do it for them and their family and apparently that's enough for them to be experts in the area. They think they are being useful nit picking on your techniques.

Umm no, you're not honey, you're irritating my ethnic nerves ... go outside and do some pretend male activity and be useful away from me while I clean, please…..

Yes we are crazy ethnic chicks and we are our own worst enemy!

Sometimes we ease up on ourselves and relax a bit and breathe for a day or so and slow the pace down and maybe not use the washing machine for one day and tell ourselves that its ok to rest a bit and not be so frantic all the time, then bang! My child is yelling at me: "Where is that black t-shirt I wore yesterday? Is it washed yet mum? I need it now! I've got nothing else to wear! OMG nothing of mine is ever ready. Mum, why are you not answering me?"

Oh shit, the mum guilt now creeps in: "Calm down, I will organise it now for you sweetheart. Give me ten minutes. I can do a quick wash and dry for you if you think you absolutely have nothing else to wear in that entire jam-packed cupboard of yours! Mother Mary help me please!" (The religious references and cry for help, another Italian trait).

See what happens when I take my foot off the pedal to breathe and take time to relax? THIS is what happens. One day there will be time to breathe or time to do my own things. Haven't got time to slow down now. Just listen to them complain.

We place so many obligations and expectations on ourselves that we don't give ourselves the chance to live a life full of memories. We pressure ourselves and never stop until we drop. I'm not sure if the dropping of exhaustion at the end of the night is when we finally give ourselves permission to tell ourselves we did well.

Giussa, I'm here to tell you, you have always done well! Give yourself some time to breathe and enjoy your successes! Not simply push for more and more. Your worth in this world is not dependent on you doing things perfectly. Your worth is what shines from your eyes when you laugh and smile and be your true self and you're surrounded by your kids, husband, family and friends, having a great time.

Start by being your true awesome self! Get out of the bloody kitchen and laundry; go and do something for yourself. Be adventurous! Enough now.

You are ENOUGH as you are.

You DO ENOUGH.

GO LIVE YOUR BEST LIFE FOR YOU!

What Is the Cost of These Obligations?

The cost is we are trying to fulfil this perfect life and we are not really sure what that actually is, and we just end up experiencing the grind of life that exhausts us to the core. Why do we strive and kill ourselves so much for success and for material things when in fact we never grew up this way?

We want too much in our life – we aspire to much more than what our parents and grandparents did when they migrated to Australia. My parents just wanted safety and a good life that allowed them the opportunity to work and live a happy life with more opportunities for their children. Our parents' generations were more resilient than us and their life was harder due to their language skills. They wanted less than us and in some cases I think they were happier than us. But they also created this life for us growing up with too many rules and obligations and judgements of what is the right way of doing things and the wrong way of doing things. They did it for us to try and keep us safe and together and ensure we had high standards in life, but they set the standards so high that we thought we had to not only meet but exceed them.

The pressure that we experience ourselves is probably due to our own ambition to be better than our parents, however I feel they laughed and connected with their family more than we do. They were not perfect; they did their best and they saved up for new things and holidays away. My parents never threw anything out unless it stopped working or was no longer functional. The chairs that were upgraded inside then went outside as outdoor chairs. Nothing at my parent's house was 'matchy-matchy' and that was ok. We change our furnishings and upgrade them on a whim, just because we fall in love with something at Harvey Norman one Sunday afternoon. Even our kettle or toaster at home was only thrown out when it stopped working, not because another style or colour would look better. My dad would often not replace things when they broke down so we grew up being very careful with our possessions as there was no guarantee that they would be replaced. You simply go without and learn to make do with what you have.

When I got married, everything in my house had to be new and match and on trend. All my friends were the same and we loved buying new items to add to our proud home. My mother kindly advised me stop worrying about these type of status symbols in life and try to pay more off the mortgage so that we would have some room to breathe when the family planning started. I never listened to this and had a very enjoyable life spending all my earnings on home items, socialising, dinners and holidays. I thought it was that my mother simply lived a boring and frugal Italian life. Unfortunately, when I finally had my child, I had to return to work quicker than expected and miss out on things with my only child, Marcus. So yes, she was right. I didn't have the luxury of staying home as my mortgage was still high. I had a good time though....living the dream for a while.

I think the perception of what is value for money changes from generation to generation. You would be surprised the amount of arguments we have had with my son over ordering UBER eats. John screams out constantly: "Make yourself a bloody sandwich and stop wasting money on UBER eats and crap food … there is free bread and mortadella in the fridge!"

"I don't feel like mortadella, Dad," Marcus would answer. "I feel like sushi."

OMG we are sounding like our parents! What have we become? God help us!

My dad would say the same thing to us growing up about Hungry Jacks. In fact I never had a Whopper until I was in my late teens and paid for it with my own money. It was very much frowned upon in our household as a waste of money and not necessary when we had so much good food at home to eat. Take away only consisted of a bought cooked chicken once a week and never any chips. My parents would make the chips themselves at home for us. "There are plenty of potatoes in the pantry to peel," my mother would remind us.

The flip side recently has been when we attend a simple family lunch at our parents' we feel so happy and enjoy the rustic food and family around us, especially all the kids in the family. There is no pressure and we don't care that everything is not styled, or that the plates and settings are not perfectly matching. We simply attend and enjoy ourselves and make do at Nonna and Nonno's house with whatever they have on hand. The old kitchen chairs are still outside as spare outdoor chairs, the garden has tomato plants held up with old re-used sticks and the patio area is filled with different sizes of odd pot plants with cuttings that my mum has stolen from her neighbourhood walks from other people's gardens. We all love spending time there in the rustic garden that is a combination of different colours and eras. So why have we changed the scenario so much for ourselves and our family and home? Why so much pressure on ourselves and our generation?

This perfection strategy we are all implementing is now having an effect on our beloved children. They see us seek perfection and believe that this is the only way to do things in life. They feel that they have to be perfect successful beings like their parents and have everything look perfect, have perfect bedrooms or homes and be perfect, otherwise they are failures in life. Even worse, they do not even try something unusual for the fear of failing. They step away from opportunities due to fear. And to their detriment we are there always ready to catch them because we also enable their lack of resilience. Sometimes as parents we get too cautious with them and their feelings, that we do not teach them to reach too high. We fear their reaction as they may might fall or fail and then we can't catch or help them.

Their resilience in life is even less than ours when we were young ourselves. Furthermore they have become more anxious beings compared to our generation. Precious and sensitive to everything in the world at times. This then causes us as parents to be anxious just watching them be anxious.

An example of this was my son during COVID, when we were staying at home in lockdown for 10 days in Adelaide. He was complaining how restricted and bored he felt and was questioning when it was going to get back to normal so that he could get out of this house and see his friends to hang out and to buy his beloved sushi and cold rolls. Apparently this lock down was killing him.

I responded to him: "It's only been a week, my child. You try staying home every day for the entire three-month summer school holidays and not being allowed to go past the back gate, with your parents at work all day, not feeding and preparing constant food for you and not having an endless supply of snacks. Your days were spent with your sisters to hang with and only having books or TV to watch. There were no play dates and we had chores to do every day. That is how I grew up my entire Australian-Italian childhood until I was at least 17. This COVID is nothing mate, get some resilience in you! Use your brain and keep yourself occupied: read a bloody book or I can give you some cleaning chores to do! Growing up an ethnic chick in a strict family is harder than COVID, I am telling you!"

In my case I was not allowed to do most things and dreamed of the freedom I thought non-ethnic children enjoyed. My child is not ruled by the same strictness yet will not put himself out there with all of the opportunities that come his way. No matter what I say or tell him how lucky he has it compared to my upbringing, there is still no reaction or movement forward. I really struggle with this and yet I feel that the more I pressure him, the more anxious he will get and then this causes other issues like low self-esteem and confidence.

I get sad for all his missed opportunities in life and get anxious about his social development and future. "Be brave my child," is all I want to say to him. "Life is a journey, not a destination; be confident and use your strong wings to soar high like an eagle! Aim high, look up and dream big!" However the reality is that we are not our kid's gatekeepers in life. Our children must all experience their own journey and we should not live our own lives through our kids.

Our parents did this to us to a certain degree and I feel that this was to our detriment, as we were always looking back over our shoulder checking whether they approved and we were making them proud. The big problem with our parents is that they didn't have the skills or language ability to tell us. In fact if you didn't get the negative response you had to assume that you were on the right track.

We cannot repeat the same mistakes our parents made, by trying to control our children's journey in an attempt to keep them safe and within our reach. We also cannot raise our children the same way our parents raised us - they raised us in a world that no longer exists.

Recently I was doing the same in my life. Where is my bravery to try new opportunities and develop myself outside my comfort zone? Trying out a new brand of washing powder or a new recipe for my family does not count as effective development skills or living my best life, growing outside my comfort zone or ensuring that I don't have any regrets in life before I get too old.

Competitive Women

All women can be bitchy and we are all good at congregating in little groups making comments and judgements about things and people around us. Ethnic females are usually very friendly and will always greet each other with the obligatory kiss on the cheek. I have many wonderful ethnic women friends in my life. However, I also feel that as a cultural group we are also very judgemental and competitive. Possibly that's because we have grown up in our homes and community being judged and being rewarded as pretty little things and we simply slip into that negativity and comparative tactic when we don't feel good about ourselves.

Some of the nicest women I know I have seen with my own eyes turn into competitive nasty women at events, judging other accomplished women based on their looks alone. Universally as women we are all judged on our looks and how well we look at our age, especially how sexy we are to our men folk. Ethnic women are very passionate, proud women and many love the male attention. I would think that all women at some stage in our lives put aside that competition with other women for looks and maintaining their weight. Why do we women become competitive on this external level? Let's lift each other up and let's focus both on the good we women have achieved in our lives as individuals and whether we are actually a good and kind person on the inside and towards others. Let's look at women's achievements in the workplace or within their homes nurturing their children and themselves.

This aesthetic judgement based on what competitive women perceive as perfection almost invariably has consequences on their quality of life and towards other women and girls in society. When we expect everything and everyone to be perfect including ourselves, we not only distort what is beautiful, but we create a cruel world where people personal qualities are overlooked and flaws are heightened.

I am personally aware that within our culture, women are not often openly praised or acknowledged for our great achievements in the workplace and we are not rewarded for being ambitious and running businesses. Many of these skills are seen as more masculine traits and women are acknowledged for our feminine aspects such as our looks, how we nurture our family - and in the Italian community - how well we cook those traditional dishes and all aspects of food. All women are different and we should celebrate our diversity in skill sets rather than try to compete and tear each other down.

Still a Proud Giussa Today

I am a proud Giussa. I lived and breathed this persona in my teenage years and beyond. Older and like-minded Giussa and Mario's are still the same people I associate with and see regularly today. We have our groups of people that we all met all those years ago in our twenties and we still are friends despite our busy lives and distant catch ups. We are mostly all married now with our own families, some divorced and some single. Essentially we are still the same people and still have those deep connections and memories that we developed as young people together. We still gather together in groups at our homes and at various outings and we still have the same innocent fun together, lots of banter and human contact. This is what I love about our ethnic generation, we are the same people: just wiser, older and now greyer.

After my dad died suddenly from a heart attack in July 2020, I had an overwhelming feeling that all those rules I adhered to were now invalid and never really made a difference in this world. He controlled me and I dutifully obeyed as he expected I would. In his mind he was in control of his daughters and family, they reflected what person he was. Then once we married, our husbands were there to take over directing our path forward. That was the way it was: the traditional Italian way or was it just what my dad thought was the way for his girls? We were the support people, the doers, the work horses of the family being protected, guided and helped to feel safe by our men folk.

Was it that my dad simply didn't understand his daughters? I often wondered if it was only his lack of clarity? Or was it like that for all women my age and within my cultural group at that time?

Did he not realise that I didn't need anyone to tell me what my path should be like and that I am quite capable and confident to stand shoulder to shoulder with any male of my generation, including my husband? I am also quite capable of making informed and intelligent decisions, including financial ones. I also have the ability to run a household and hold down a career, and actually have an intelligent conversation at a dinner party and serve the food at the same time.

Was it only my dad that thought me safer or in better hands with the constant guidance of a male person in my life to ensure that my journey would be on the best and safest path in life?

Part Five

Evolving: Embracing a New Chapter

At the age of 25 I read a life changing book called *Feel the Fear and Do It Anyway* by Susan Jeffers.

This book was about overcoming fears, healing the pain and moving forward with things in your life. Once I read it, I felt like it spoke to me on a personal level. At that age I had acknowledged that all the conforming and restrictions in my life felt at times like invisible chains around my neck and I was tired of feeling powerless. I was powerless waiting to be married; I was powerless and unable to travel with my partner and I was powerless and preferred not to go against my family cultural rules. I simply wanted to feel energised and enthusiastic about life and actively achieving goals for my own mental health and self-esteem.

"Go on Giussa," I would say to myself. "See if you can do this new adventure or job title. Do not fear the unknown or the prospect of failing; be courageous and brave to try and maybe you might just succeed … and if you don't then another path will be there for you." It is not the failure in our life that defines us, it is the moments when we decide to get back up after failure that really defines our strength and what matters in life.

The two areas I focused on reaching and daring myself outside my comfort zone was my career and the new job roles I actively changed to learn and achieve more and adventurous activities to get my spirit racing and feel the thrill of it all.

I was always very adventurous and sporty and I decided that it was time to set some serious adventure goals and get my heart beat racing and push myself outside my comfort zone. I vowed to "feel the fear and do it anyway."

I quietly felt that if I pursued life this way, then one day I would be brave enough to completely break from the chains I felt from conforming as a *Good Italian Girl* and lead my own life without worrying about the judgements and guilt that constantly surrounded me.

I firstly started listing all the things I wanted to achieve in all areas of my life and created a "Bucket List" of goals. No goal was too ridiculous to achieve. I have maintained this list ever since I was 25 years old in a little black book constantly adding, reviewing and picking each goal listed, then setting myself a certain time frame in which to achieve it. Most of my adventures were once off events and I was able to cross them off the list as achieved. Some were harder to achieve than others but it was essentially about the act of trying something new and being challenged; not being perfect and over analysing the risks. I loved ticking off things on my bucket list: not just adventurous things but a simple event like trying a new restaurant or a different type of food. These things also allow me to grow and learn and be outside my comfort zone and develop as a person to become the best version of myself.

Some of the specific adventure items I started with during my mid 20's and 30's were: tandem skydiving, abseiling, bungee jumping, gliding, white water rafting, jet boating, rock climbing, beach horse riding, mustering cattle on a horse, jet skiing, water skiing, sailing, boogie boarding, go karting/luge and mountain climbing. In my 40's I continued with several snorkelling events (these were big achievements as I fear deep water), zip lining, bridge climbs in Sydney and New Zealand and walking charity events. My goals for my 50's have just started, with two very big bucket list items achieved already with the establishment of my new business called Shining Light and becoming an international bestselling published author. Most recently I have decided to take dancing lessons again and researching information on building a tiny home on land at my happy place in Middleton South Australia.

I believe that you are never too old to set another goal or dream a new dream. I want to inspire people to connect with others, dream big and live kinder.

The Start Of My Transformation

As predicted most transformations start with some definitive event that makes you wake up and take note.

I thought my long and personally traumatic IVF journey was my event that would make me look at the world from a different perspective, which I did and I thought, "hey fair's fair, I did the infertility struggle for almost two decades and now its someone's else's shot universe … I'm all good here … My turn for only the good things. I know how lucky I am in life and I am grateful for what I have and I'm ready just to see the sunshine now … no more darkness or crying for me anymore … got nothing left in me, I'm all used up."

Well, obviously not. The universe or fate decided to really test my Giussa resilience and give me a tumour scare at the age of 48. There I was, working hard within my business and kicking some real financial goals. My confidence was high with my growing client base and referrals and I finally felt a real sense of achievement and purpose. I was ready to move forward and be positive and dream big.

Whoa Claudia, hang on a minute.

Giussa, let me introduce you to the world of MRI scanning and PET scanning and CT scanning every 6 months, then on a yearly cycle. The specialists were clueless as to how I somehow returned from a flight home from Sydney experiencing head pain and pulsating tinnitus. I apparently had a small 'glomus jugulare tumour' at the base of my skull that somehow appeared or was always there all my life. No specialist could tell me the actual reason and if it would grow or affect me long term. I was in no way prepared for another bump in the road and again the feel of a chain around my neck, but this time with an unknown condition. I simply couldn't solve it and the operation to discover what it was could result in more damage to my hearing and possible facial paralysis on my left side.

The unknown had again surfaced in my life and I felt the real thoughts of my mortality and time wasted doing things that were not making me happy. I was thinking about my legacy and how many years I might have left in the world.

I started wondering how long will I betray my calling or inner truth for the easier option?

The fact was that despite having a successful business, I really wanted the chance to start something to empower women also going through IVF and who are struggling with being brave and going after what they want in their life. I want myself and other women and their children to have the courage to find what their soul is searching for. These thoughts would encircle me for a few more years before I would really start seeing life through a new lens … a sort of kaleidoscope.

Kaleidoscopes

Life is under no obligation to deliver what you expect in this world and I didn't expect any of the paths - good and bad - that I had travelled along so far. Now I felt was my chance to change direction or curve it slightly and change my mindset. Like a kaleidoscope I started unlocking parts of myself that had been waiting for me to find and show the world my leadership skills and be the voice who starts the difficult conversations.

The *Change Makers* opportunity entered my life at the right time as I felt that I had the courage to speak my truth and write about the effects of infertility and IVF treatments no matter how hard it was going to be.

I am incredibly honoured and grateful to (publisher) Emma Hamlin for helping me to become a bestselling author and I was excited about the opportunity of changing the stereotypes and stigma around infertility and IVF.

The opportunity to be part of *Change Makers Volume 4* made me simply step up and be real, without any mask. I felt notable changes in myself during this time of writing my contribution for the book, having a book launch in Adelaide and seeing women purchase my book for themselves and friends. At the book launch I had several one-on-one conversations with women about their own infertility journeys with IVF and miscarriage. Most of them admitted that they didn't share this grief or stress with others as they felt no one understood. They thanked me for sharing my journey and said they wished they had opened up about their own stories, to help themselves heal. I felt that my writing and messages made a real impact in other people's lives and helped me realise that a new path was emerging. I was actually empowering other women to be their authentic selves and to be brave enough to take chances in stepping up and being more present in their lives for themselves. I truly felt I was and could make a real impact in other people's lives. I was still myself emerging from a cocoon of my former self and beliefs, and felt like there were no limits to the extent of the transformation that is possible for me.

Establishing My New Business Shining Light

At 50 years old I held a joint 50th birthday celebration with my fellow amazing ethnic Giussa bestie, Gina. One of my main reasons I wanted to have a big birthday celebration with Gina was to celebrate our beautiful and supportive friendship just like we did at our joint 30th birthday party, twenty years prior. Also, on a personal level in some way celebrate the start of a new perspective on life and acknowledging to myself that it was in fact time to move on to other things in life and be grateful for what I had already achieved. It was an amazing and fun event, despite some people's behaviour.

After this event I felt this recurring theme of women not supporting other women was circling back in my space and around me for me to take note of... why? I had this overwhelming feeling of doing something about it in some unique way. I wanted to somehow encourage women to be more supportive of each other, be kinder and to encourage and empower themselves and their children. To be positive in their approach to life despite the difficult times in life. I knew how hard it was to overcome a difficult journey without success and I personally had used many techniques such as journalling and affirmations to help me stay positive and motivated along the way.

I followed my instincts and took a leap of faith that I could personally be a positive influence on others, just as I had done professionally in my life as a training facilitator. I could help other women feel empowered and supported and develop resilience.

This was how Shining Light was born. My next instinct was to ask my forever chaperone in life – my sister Diana - to join me and run this new side business with me. We work hard in it together through our love of inspiring women and children in this world to be their unique selves and having the confidence to overcome any challenge that life throws at them.

At Shining Light, the core range of our business is selling gratitude journals, positive affirmation cards and motivational products for women and children. Our aim is help others believe in their inner strength and to love and accept themselves and others just the way they are. Our message is simple:

- We believe that when one shines, we all shine.
- Be grateful for what you have in life. Start each day with a grateful heart, there are so many beautiful reasons to be happy.
- Live your best life.
- Be kind to yourself and others.
- Be your awesome authentic self and be true to yourself.
- You are enough as you are.
- Never stop dreaming and let your dreams be your wings.
- Have happy thoughts and use positive affirmations daily.

- Believe that you are never too old to start something new or have a new adventure.
- Acknowledge that life is complicated and that you have to learn to be happy now and not wait for things to get better.
- Be resilient, everything you need is already within you.
- You have the inner strength and courage to overcome any challenge.
- Accept yourself for who you are and ignore the negative comments from others.

Death, Italians and Regrets

Death and Italians can be written in the same sentence. We worry about dying and think we are all going to die young. When we hear someone is sick or dying we automatically do the internal panic and wonder if something bad is going to happen to us or someone close to us. We are very anxious people and over thinkers. We try not talk about death too much as we then think we are going to jinx ourselves and actually get sick or die.

Some examples of regular discussions friends have had with me:

"I felt a pain in my arm today at work, maybe it's a sign of a stroke."

"I have this terrible headache, what are the warning signs of an aneurism?"

"Did you hear such and such was diagnosed with cancer ….poor bloke. It's happening all around me."

When most of us think about death and people getting a disease, we automatically have this feeling that we should slow our own life down, stop stressing and stop worrying about the small things in life and go out and fulfill some of our dreams. We think about taking time out to connect with the ones we love and do the things that bring us joy and happiness. We all believe that we have time to reach those bucket list goals and dreams in life. However sometimes life is cruel and not as we have planned and we lose those opportunities and take up time in our lives doing insignificant tasks. What we need to do is make sure we don't have any regrets in life by reaching those bucket list goals.

Recently my recurring thoughts have been: *Claudia, get your act together and go out and get shit done and live a bit, work less before it's too late.* However, most people just ponder on the idea of changing things in their life, and simply go on with life talking about their symptoms and never really changing.

Changing is hard for Italians as they are so set in their ways and they are also quite stubborn. They all think they are right: I can say that because I am Australian-Italian.

We ethnic women and Giussas always think we have time on our hands. I hear so many of us having discussions (including myself) about one day I will have time to do something for myself: I just have to wait until things are less hectic, or until the kids reach a certain age, or I will wait a little more before I go on a special holiday with my husband without the kids but we should pay off a little more of this, or save for that, or buy our child this desperately wanted gadget as I want them to be happy. My childhood was not much fun and I want my kids to have a fun and eventful childhood and look after their needs first. Blah, blah, we are always "gonna", are we not?

Well, NOT THIS GIUSSA and YOU can change as well.

It's time to take action now Giussa before it's too late!

I want you to close your eyes and imagine that you're at your own big ethnic funeral. Your family is carrying or following the coffin down the middle of the church all dressed in black, crying, head down (well, hopefully they are crying). A bit morbid, I know, but you won't jinx yourself. There's a good reason for it. Now think about what you'd like people to say about you. What kind of life do you want to lead? People die with all kinds of regrets. Don't be one of them. This is some of them as a reminder to try to change some aspects of your life if you can now. Yes, now, not later in your life!

Recently after hearing of another female my age and her sad cancer diagnosis, I decided to do a bit of Googling and work out the biggest thing people regret before they die. I came across an article in the Guardian where a palliative nurse named Bronnie Ware who has counselled the dying in their last days, revealed the top five regrets of the dying:

1. **I wish I'd had the courage to live a life true to myself, not the life others expected of me.**

"This was the most common regret of all. When people realise that their life is almost over and look back clearly on it, it is easy to see how many dreams have gone unfulfilled. Most people had not honoured even a half of their dreams and had to die knowing that it was due to choices they had made, or not made. Health brings a freedom very few realise, until they no longer have it."

2. I wish I hadn't worked so hard.

"This came from every male patient that I nursed. They missed their children's youth and their partner's companionship. Some deeply regretted spending so much of their lives on the treadmill of a work existence."

3. I wish I'd had the courage to express my feelings.

"Many people suppressed their feelings in order to keep peace with others. As a result, they settled for a mediocre existence and never became who they were truly capable of becoming. Many developed illnesses relating to the bitterness and resentment they carried as a result."

4. I wish I had stayed in touch with my friends.

"Often they would not truly realise the full benefits of old friends until their dying weeks and it was not always possible to track them down. Many had become so caught up in their own lives that they had let golden friendships slip by over the years. There were many deep regrets about not giving friendships the time and effort that they deserved. Everyone misses their friends when they are dying."

5. I wish that I had let myself be happier.

"This is a surprisingly common one. Many did not realise until the end that happiness is a choice. They had stayed stuck in old patterns and habits. The so-called 'comfort' of familiarity overflowed into their emotions, as well as their physical lives. Fear of change had them pretending to others, and to their selves, that they were content, when deep within, they longed to laugh properly and have silliness in their life again."

What's your greatest regret so far and what will you set out to achieve or change before you die? If I was to die right now my answer would be:

➢ I wish I'd had the courage to live a life true to myself, not the life others expected of me.

➢ I wish I'd had the courage to express my feelings.

➢ I wish that I had let myself be happier.

➢ I wish I hadn't worried so much.

➢ I wish I'd cared less about what other people think.

➢ I wish I'd taken better care of myself and my health.

➢ I wish I'd travelled more.

I realised that nothing listed above was remotely related to material possessions such as the new house and car I have wanted to upgrade now that I am over 50.

After writing this book, and the journey it has taken me on, I believe that I can cross off at least four of the seven items listed. COVID has cut my travel options at the moment, however, that will change over the next few years. Taking care of my health will be an ongoing process as I overcome the dislike of attending medical appointments due to the long IVF fertility process and more recent tumour scare.

Today is the day you stop just existing and start living your dying bucket list. Let's do it together, Giussas!

Don't waste your time in regret, anger and worries. Life is too short to be unhappy.

I have designed some special tools for my readers to start thinking about their own legacy, vision and bucket list dreams in life.

Please visit my website: **www.ShiningLightcd.com.au** *to download your own free PDF copies* and start your own transformational journey and legacy for your family.

I will be forever grateful for my Messenger conversation with Melanie Spring from the USA: her Instagram story caught my eye one day as I sat in the car crying about life a few weeks after my dad passed. She was promoting her training program: "I Speak with Confidence." She messaged me her encouragement and told me: "Everyone has a story to tell the world: only the truly brave will stand up and share it". I signed up for the training program, ready to gain knowledge in speaking, and help to prepare a script about my IVF story. It was at that very moment that I decided to start promoting my IVF story that I had written and only circulated locally, to a wider audience and speak out about my journey.

It was time to stand up and do something. Then the universe sent me Emma Hamlin and the *Change Makers* opportunity. Big thanks and love to Melanie. I also thank the universe that I connected with you, and I am now part of your Melanie Spring's Rock stars and Kick Ass Humans Club.

Melanie Spring's key message is to:

- Decide what it is you want
- Write it down
- Make a plan
- Work on it every single day
  #Manifestthatshit

Think of something you want to do right now and ask yourself what is it? You are probably too scared to take the leap and just do it – you will probably overthink it and think of all the things that are stopping you.

It is fear talking – fear of failure and yes, I can relate to it, these are the negative habits we have been taught by those around us and also our own fearful negativity. We spend our entire lives being surrounded by them and practising them.

Let's let go of any fear, shame or guilt around the direction of living our best lives. Let's act from inspiration, not obligation. The world wants to open up a huge door of joy, love and abundance and all we need to do is surrender and allow every bit of divine energy to envelop us fully, deep into our soul and hearts.

While we are talking about what people would say at your funeral, let's just go a bit deeper shall we Giussa, and talk about our strengths, accomplishments and values in life.

People often struggle to identify their strengths. Even if they do figure out what makes them special, they may then have trouble highlighting and acknowledging them to anyone or sometimes feel shameful in saying it out loud or promoting themselves. Italians don't like people with big egos and bragging about their accomplishments in a loud and showy manner. We are a very humble culture, and in fact, I believe that our culture often downplays our accomplishments when others tell us how good we are when we have achieved something. This is done by both men and women I have observed.

We ethnic, Giussa women are definitely not good at all at acknowledging our strengths out loud or even to ourselves. This I believe is part of our cultural conditioning. Being loud and confident was not something encouraged by our families or if it was, it was only in certain areas of our lives. I have noticed that we can acknowledge and can be loud and confident about our cooking, our children and cleaning skills. I think these are areas we are often applauded for and we were encouraged to be confident about with our family and friends. I can remember hearing my fellow ethnic women family members proudly boast about their beautiful lasagnes or the zeppole which they proclaim are the best in the family. For the record I never boast about my cooking but I can hold my own and I do have a good reputation of having great parties with lots of atmosphere and well co-ordinated table decor (just saying). This type of confidence is what we do naturally as ethnic women and often we feel even more special and have an immense sense of pride when our husbands and children confirm it out loud to the world, especially to our peers.

Cooking and cleaning are great ethnic female skills and are useful skills to have in life. But what about the rest of your skills, Giussa? I know how awesome you are and the other skills you have developed in your life and the accomplishments you have achieved. I personally know how hard it is to talk about my awesomeness and my accomplishments. I also have never been able to promote myself unless I am going to a job interview and even then it is a real struggle to really be super confident and sell myself without being courageous.

If you were to go back in time and give yourself a message what would it be, Giussa? Are you showing up in your life with all you've got? In a world where you can be anything, don't be scared to try. Dare to dream big!

Come on, let's reflect on our accomplishments and tell ourselves out loud how truly special we are and gain some confidence. Let's list 3 key skills that make us all awesome and uniquely us. Share with me the following and write them down for reference later:

- What's your unique superpower?
- What differentiates you from others?
- What are you proud of?

If this is hard to do, you can also seek external help or ask your family and friends. Text three people and ask them: what makes me fabulous? Reflect on what they say about you, your skills and the unique value you bring to your work or friendships.

Maybe we all need to implement an accomplishment journal. Let's write down an accomplishment at the end of each workday. With 5 days in the week and 52 weeks in the year, you will have 260 accomplishments in a single year!

Outside of recognising our accomplishments, it is difficult to act in alignment with your values if you don't know what they are. Values are at the core of who we are, it is the lens through which we see life and find purpose. We often think of our values and respond with "my kids and my career." Let's dig a bit deeper, Giussa. Some questions can help you identify what matters to you the most.

- What are the things that really matter to me as a person?
- What is my definition of living my best life and during which activities do I feel most inspired?
- What new things and adventures would I like to pursue?
- Who are the people you relate well to and align with: who makes you laugh out loud?

If this task is difficult, maybe seek external help and think about those who know you well: what values would they attribute to you? Alternatively what are the top 3 comments you have received that reflect who you believe you are?

I have often thought that values are simply ingrained. However, we do actually have the ability to change some of our old and traditional belief systems. It is possible to be open to new ways of thinking and behaving, yet still be grounded by our fundamental values: just not be restrained by them. When we instil values and by allowing ourselves this flexibility, we allow ourselves to grow.

How Have I Personally Redefined the Unwritten Italian Rule Book?

Stop looking for approval - you are enough as you are - your future self is waiting for you

Approval and growth do not mix together. If you want to grow you need to be willing to let go of the sea of approval. Let go of the old you that you see in the mirror and the limiting voices in your head screaming that you are not good enough. Grow, let go, create a new relationship with yourself and others. Do not be afraid to start all over again. Your new story might be a better one. Find out what you really want, embrace your unique you and become a more powerful version of yourself.

Reset mindset program - let go of the old rules and make new ones - unlearn - rethink

Reset and remove your limiting beliefs based on your cultural upbringing and those instilled by our parents. Put the brakes on the ancestral trauma and step into your real self. Lower the bar and give yourself a break. We work so hard to please others. Why do we worry so much? Why do we work so hard for no acknowledgement? Break free from limiting beliefs. When you become different, the world responds to you differently. Please visit our website: www.ShiningLightcd.com.au to view our motivational self-paced workbooks on positivity and mindset available to purchase.

A line in the sand – find a new path and direction – life on your terms

Where does the judgement come from? Remove the judgement towards yourself and others and you will become free. Learn to recognise those past "locked in" behaviours and memory and create new behaviours. My dad passing was like a final trigger that prompted me to let go and find my own way of doing things: to trust my instincts and live life my own way. A clearing of the pathways.

Develop a self-growth plan- Shine Bright – Goal setting the key to success and happiness

Do not shrink yourself so as to be more palatable to the world. Stop apologising for who you are. What are your success blockers? Start thinking of what you have and what you always wanted. Have courage to speak your mind and stand up for your own beliefs. You are not only here to serve others and be put to the side. Ask yourself what's really important and then have the wisdom and courage to build your life around your answers. Allow yourself to be that woman you want to be. Be visible, be engaging and amplify your magnetic presence and bring your best self forward.

Choice of Possibility - Do not be fearful - Be curious and explore - Spread your wings

Give yourself an opportunity to go beyond your comfort zone. Choosing to do something new for yourself will give you more joy. Choice takes us beyond what is currently stopping us. Your new awareness can truly change you and how you see your world around you.

Focus on what's important for your children

Remember as pregnant mothers we carried a child into the world with unlimited potential. They were gifts from the moment they were born. Let's inspire our children and give them choices. Talk to them like they are infinite beings and allow them to be everything that they are. Don't suppress them in any way and take the judgement out of parenting. You don't need to be perfect to inspire your children. We are not our children's gatekeepers in life. Our children need unconditional belonging to grow into self-acceptance. Years from now you want to be able to say you were the mum your kids always needed. Focus on what's important.

Never stop learning new things - love what you do - be a leader in your own life - make yourself a priority. Live a life of abundance

Learn leadership skills and be a great leader for yourself and your family. Empower yourself and learn to be confident, resilient and optimistic. Never stop learning new things so that you can lead effectively. Pass on the best of who you are to your children. Never stop learning: our children deserve smart parents. Thrive to exceed the expectations of our mind.

Expand in abundance. Set your intentions. Abundance means you are connecting with who you are meant to be. Inspire change and create wealth. Reconcile your fears of failure and live your soul's mission. What are you really scared of? Not everyone is going to understand what you're doing – do it anyway. We have to learn to be okay with our own vision. Don't let it affect you. Dream Big Now. Stop waiting for things before you change. Strip away everything that is holding you back and have freedom to make your own choices.

Self-love notes - nurture yourself - step into your own worth - heal yourself

Create your own self love and love the person you were and the person you fought to become. Use mantras or quotes to inspire yourself daily. A negative mind will never give you a positive life. It's time to ditch that negative voice in your head for good. Act from a place of self-worth. Listen to your heart, it will always bring you home. Please visit our website: www.ShiningLightcd.com.au to view our diverse range of affirmation cards available to purchase.

Breathe; Be Grateful & Find your Balance

Learn some breathing exercises to assist in creating a positive energy around you. Learn some clearing statements. Practice the concept of gratitude and journal your thoughts daily. Mediate and ground yourself daily and just be. Be Mindful. Live in the moment. Please visit our website: www.ShiningLightcd.com.au to view our diverse range of gratitude journals for women and children available to purchase.

Connect with others - Find your tribe, your soul sisters in life

I call this the "ethnic soul sister connection" or "tribe" or "ethnic women circle". Connect with women around you, reconnect with your old tribe or be brave and find a new connection. We as women need that mutual supportive connection in this world with other like-minded women who are honest, supportive, understanding and who are not jealous or competitive.

Let's shine and connect together. Join my VIP Facebook group - The Good Italian Girl and Giussa. This page will update you on up-and-coming network meetings and special events.

What Is the "Ethnic Soul Sister Connection?"

Have you ever met someone in your life where you did a double-take and felt that this person must either be related or definitely your soul sister? She was sort of a Giussa like me but a lot tougher in her convictions and opinions on social justice but also so caring and thoughtful. Surely there can't be another person on this planet that I can totally resonate with and completely connect to? She had a similar sassy nature combined with a sharp, quick-witted sense of humour. Yep, I found her at my sister's friend's picnic the summer before university started for both of us. My bestie girlfriend Gina and I had a divine "Scorpion" connection at our first encounter some 30 years ago and I have been grateful for our encounter ever since.

We always laugh together and have very real, honest supportive conversations. We have often shared similar lessons and had very similar experiences growing up as strong, opinionated yet respectful ethnic females within our strict families. Through connection and awareness of what we each represent within this world we have created what I like to call an "ethnic chicks bond".

Gina is not the only ethnic chick I have bonded with over the years and felt the soul sister connections on this planet. There are so many and I feel very fortunate in my life to have them surrounding me on a daily basis. This is in addition to the fortunate feeling of being born within a family of girls and having regular gatherings with my three sisters.

This "ethnic soul sister connection" or "tribe" or "ethnic women circle" is another area I talk about with other women with similar backgrounds and many are fortunate to also have this connection in their lives. We as women need that mutual supportive connection in this world with other like-minded women who are honest, supportive, understanding and who are not jealous or competitive.

I can recall regular conversations with many "ethnic soul sisters" over the years discussing the very things I am writing about. We have laughed out loud, cried and felt the mutual frustrations of our lives that we have had to deal with many similar issues of simply trying to be our unique, authentic selves. Many of us tried to live our lives our own way within the ethnic obligations faced by women born within our era. Just like our ethnic mothers we have tried to be the heart and soul for our children, partners and parents, yet unlike our mothers we have also dedicated the same drive and passion to developing our own careers and having our own interests at the same time. The juggle is more real than they ever experienced in their era and the mother/ wife/daughter guilt is at times very overwhelming, combined with the mental and emotional exhaustion.

Giussa, if you take anything away from this book of mine it is the recommendation to start being part of a circle or further develop and connect with the circle you have around you. Please do not neglect it; make time in your life to nurture the connection with other women. I feel that as women, we need this support in our lives, and I feel it is just as important as the connection we have with our husbands, children and our families. As we age our children leave the nest, parents pass away or partners are no longer with us, and support provided by other like-minded women will help with our mental health. This type of connection can come in all different shapes and sizes and new connections can happen at any stage of your life and with multiple groups of people.

I feel very strongly about this as I have seen my mum on her own since my dad's passing. I am so grateful that despite my dad's illness with early-onset dementia, she made time for herself to still connect and attend her "women's coffee group catch up" at the local shopping centre once a week over the past several years. Some weeks she didn't attend as it was overwhelmingly difficult. At times caring for my father and his lack of enthusiasm for her attending and the guilt he placed on her for leaving their home for an hour stopped her from going.

This group simply sit, drink coffee and chat and support each other. They were there supporting my mother and checking on her during and after my dad's funeral. She also connects with women around the neighbourhood for daily 7am walks. My mother is social and still an active person at the age of 79 years old. However, she did most things in life with my father side by side. She had been with my father since she was 16 years old and all her sisters and immediate family are in Belgium or have also passed away. We as her female children are there for her, however we all have work and family commitments and it is often hard for us to be there during the day with her, keeping her company to ease the loneliness. My mother reminds us that we have our own stressful lives to worry about, and even though she would welcome the regular daily visit, she is also understanding of the pressures of work and family as she herself was exhausted by it all. She has stated that her connections with other women along with her immediate family have all helped her stay positive and active after our dad's passing.

So Giussa, it really is being open to meeting other people and making an effort to go outside your comfort zone and try something new with someone new, a new group or making an effort with the group you are currently a part of. No excuses and no cooking and cleaning and reorganising the house and saying no to any invites of this nature. Just imagine the wonderful journey your life will take with these types of intermittent or regular catch-ups, not to mention the laughing!

My daily strategies in life

- My daily affirmations and journaling for an abundant life.
- My breathing techniques.
- Walking in nature and along the beach.
- Laughing daily … even a small giggle about something I have read or a funny quote.
- Connecting with someone I care about on a daily basis.

- Doing something daily that brings me joy ... even enjoying great coffee can achieve this for me.
- Being with my immediate and extended family without the pressure and expectations.
- Spending time with my fellow Giussa female like-minded friends, soul sisters and exploring the world together.
- Learning to see my thoughts as just thoughts and not get engaged by all of them.
- Spreading my message via Shining Light and empowering other women and children.

Discovering the Magic of Journaling and Positive Affirmations

Looking back now, I am amazed that after the five years I endured undertaking IVF I was able to maintain the momentum and keep going through all the treatments and day-to-day family life stresses. It might be my resilient, stubborn Australian-Italian background; however, I firmly believe that there was one area of my daily practice that saved a piece of my soul.

Letting go of your thoughts throughout the process is tough, surrendering to a feeling when that feeling is sadness and loss of hope that you will achieve your dream is a difficult thing.

The Dalai Lama once said: "Just one small positive thought in the morning can change your whole day."

In my early 30s I adopted a daily practice of reading positive affirmation quotes before bed and first thing in the morning before work. I then also commenced writing in a gratitude note book all the things I was grateful for in my life, despite the hardship I was facing. Expressing gratitude for things I was thankful for improved my health and happiness before I started IVF and during the treatment cycles. Practising gratitude provided me a reminder of the good things in my life and an appreciation of life in a general sense (i.e., I was still living and breathing and had a beautiful child and family). It helped release stress and left me feeling a sense of some control in my world of treatments that were pushing me towards a world that was outside my control.

Focussing my mind on things that were positive, trained me to think more positively about life. These gratitude and positive affirmation techniques combined with the concept of mindfulness meditation made me stronger. Meditation helped me rewire the paths in my mind and over time, these three things helped me to become more emotionally resilient.

Gratitude journaling, mindfulness, and meditation helped me think more clearly. It freed up my mind, increased my self-awareness and my ability to be positive and happy. Most importantly, it gave me clarity on issues, allowing me to feel calmer and more in control of my emotions.

These techniques combined with my beautiful child, family, friends and time to recover, saw me emerge from the depths of sadness with a firm resolution that I am still a valuable person within this world: with or without several children. Individuals undertaking this journey need to be kinder to themselves and seek support as it is a difficult thing to undertake without professional support in some form or other.

I realised once I was on the other side of the darkness and towards the light again that I wanted to share my knowledge with others and empower other women and children to practice the concept of gratitude, positivity, kindness and mindfulness and in some small way help others find their inner strength.

Why Write a Book About Being a Good Italian Girl and Giussa?

When I was in my early 30's I was trying to have a child and decided to do some courses to get my mind off the difficult process. I did several short art and craft courses and then another course called writing a children's book captured my attention. I thought it would be amazing to publish a story I could read to my own child, so I started writing. The book was called "Claude the Lion" and it was about resilience and not fearing failure or the perception of others and continuing on your own path and dreams. In the book, Claude the Lion failed at school and was told that he wasn't good enough to go to Lion teacher school but, against the odds succeeded in life anyway by dreaming big and living his authentic life. The story book was never published in book form; however, it is on my bucket list for one day.

Prior to turning 50 I wrote another story about going through IVF in an attempt to let go of the emotions surrounding this difficult time in my life and also to promote the concept of kindness, gratitude and resilience to other women and children.

When my IVF story was published in *Change Makers Volume 4* in 2020 and I became a published author, my life changed on the inside. I suddenly had these thoughts I wanted to express in written form.

I knew I had another story to tell that was always bubbling on the surface in my mind. A story so personal that I wasn't sure whether it was worth sharing with the world. These were the stories that my friends and I would exchange and laugh about. The ethnic way of growing up amidst all the cultural rules we had to adhere to. It was always difficult to explain to others unless you lived it yourself. We laughed about many things because they were in fact difficult emotions to talk about and they have often been pushed aside. The one common thing that most of my friends and myself were resolute in was keeping the good ethnic values we were raised with and changing the rules that were difficult and did not serve us well growing up. Most importantly talking things through with our children and being mindful that their feelings are valid and not to push them aside or ignore them.

So just as Claude the Lion succeeded in life, I - Claude the Good Italian Girl and Giussa - have also succeeded in life and been able to dream big, despite my challenges along the way.

What is My Personal Legacy?

As I age, the feeling of passing on my own legacy to my child is something I think about more regularly, especially writing about my own journey.

The lesson I learnt from my dad's passing is that I probably never knew all that he experienced in his own childhood and his feelings about his journey of life. Ironically, I never knew I had this many repressed feelings, thoughts and opinions either. Surely not enough to write an entire book!

The circumstances of my dad's passing also brought up many emotions for me, not just sadness and grief, but also regret.

My dad was rushed to hospital by ambulance with breathing difficulties and pain on Wednesday, July 8, 2020. This was in the midst of the COVID-19 pandemic sweeping the world. My mother called the family on arrival at the hospital and was fortunately allowed to stay with him by his side. Normally we would have all immediately left our workplaces to travel to the hospital to see him. However, we were told we would not be allowed to see him due to COVID restrictions in the hospital. Despite this, my older sister went to the hospital and remained in the outside waiting room for four hours to provide us regular updates via the nursing staff. The rest of us stayed close to our phones, eagerly awaiting his recovery news from my sister and mother.

After monitoring him for four hours and running several tests, his symptoms appeared to have settled, so the hospital decided to release him. My father was literally on his way out of his hospital room while my mother was signing the discharge papers when he had a major heart attack. He collapsed to the floor and was not able to be revived. According to the autopsy, his early onset dementia had affected his heart over time and he passed away at the age of 86 years old.

What still breaks my heart is that under normal circumstances we would have been able to see him during those four hours, and at least say some final words or give him a hug before he passed. I imagine he would have given me that nod that always seemed to say: "Hey, here is that stubborn daughter of mine coming, always doing things her way." That's how we rolled and that's how we loved each other.

The reality is that I had seen my dad briefly about a week prior and I was so preoccupied with other things that I did not spend more than two minutes with him before I rushed off on another task in my hectic life.

I thought a lot about legacy, last moments and last words since then, and particularly while writing this book.

As my older sister prepared my father's legacy speech and read it out in church to those who attended the funeral, I was stunned to learn some new facts about his career as a potter in Abruzzo, the effect the war had on his life as a youngster and his feelings about the meaning of a good life. My own child then reinforced that thought by telling me in the car home: "I never knew those things about Nonno and his life." My response was "I didn't know about some of them either Marcus." I was saddened to know that even though my journey with my dad was always filled with genuine love and happy family moments, there were also many memories about complying with how he thought his daughter should lead her life. I didn't want that to be the lasting memory of his legacy, so I decided to journal some of the background information about both my parents as a way of acknowledging my heritage and family journey. Much more than just a family tree of names. Some real-life memories and stories about their childhood and our childhood and what values we have shared together as a family, including favourite Italian recipes and traditions. Most importantly, what my Italian heritage means to me and how I live it in my present life now.

As a result of the funeral, I now have this strong desire to commence sharing my own journey for my child when the time comes. Hopefully, when he feels lost in this world, he will be able to reflect on how far he has come based on the journey of his ancestry and heritage.

You rarely get a second chance to change the script in life. The reality is that nature of life is change and the incidents that break us usually open and help us develop into who we were meant to be.

I acknowledge that many of the stories I have shared was what happened in that era with our parent's generations and most ethnic children my age. I couldn't really expect my father to behave differently from others similar to his generation and ethnicity. It was the way it was at that time and when you are born with those beliefs it is hard for them to change or really expect them to be open to change.

Yet change is what is on my agenda now. A change in my perception of my own life and how I act within this world. I want to change and focus on the values and traditions I loved with my own ethnic family and carry on those traditions with my immediate family. I also want to create my own unique traditions and record them for my own life's legacy.

I am happy and grateful that I can stand tall and just be myself. It has been hard to stand tall in a world where you are told to be certain way and that others want to keep you inside a familiar box or knock you down. But I can do it and I will do it. Never feel the need to listen to someone who wants to define you. Keep strong and keep trying to improve yourself to be the best version of you. I would not be an international bestselling author if I had listened to my career counsellor at high school.

Dare to Dream

The fire is back in my eyes. I am determined to embrace a new chapter in my life and grow.

Research has shown that the best thing for our mental wellbeing is to acknowledge and gradually deal with emotions rather than to ignore or suppress them. They will linger and grow and perhaps become more challenging to deal with them later. Talking through issues raised with our parents was often difficult to achieve because of both the cultural and communication barrier. Unfortunately this may have also led to some unresolved issues with my father that are only really resurfacing now that he has passed away.

Emotions that are ignored or pushed aside don't simply disappear from our system just because we don't want to feel them. Ignored emotions stay stuck in our bodies and will often show up later as physical symptoms: pain, sadness and all kind of vices and habits that don't serve us.

Unfelt emotions are energy that is blocked in our bodies that can hold us back from living the life that we truly want. When we choose to feel all our emotions and don't ignore them, they no longer have power over us.

Talking through issues and thoughts with my child I feel is one way that I have improved from my parents' approach. I have found that the misunderstanding between the both of us is subsequently less challenging to overcome and we are able to healthily move forward.

Every day I understand myself better and how I fit within the world around me. The world and each day is a gift and whatever tomorrow brings I am so grateful to see it.

Apart from being a good parent, wife, daughter and friend, I would like to be remembered as someone who helped women and children achieve their dreams and gave them the confidence and encouragement to be themselves as uniquely culturally influenced individuals.

We ethnic women need to stay curious and try new things and embrace the idea of being lifelong learners. We need to observe the world around us and find our own place in it by being our absolute authentic selves.

Above all, our own unique cultural perspectives and experiences have value for us and value for the world - including the workplace. Our unique cultural understanding and diversity has potential and a profound impact on others in ways that you may not be aware of yet or even understand.

I want each and every one of my ethnic soul sisters to find your passion, and share your innate abilities and self with the world around you. Believe in your own dreams, self-worth and be your authentic self.

I recently read about an ancient Japanese practice called "Kintsugi". This process literally means gold mending. Instead of discarding the marred vessels, practitioners of the art repair broken items with a golden adhesive that enhances the break lines, making the piece unique. As part of this art they relish the blemishes and turn these scars into art. They believe that the lines made by time and rough use are not sources of shame, and with the gold mending the beauty is emphasised through the breaks and imperfections.

Yes, that is a perfect description of my Giussa life: born into a drawer, a few missteps along the way, lots of great experiences, some failure then a bit of patchwork to those scars which in the end only emphasise my true beauty from within.

It's easy to look back and question decisions you have made in the past, but it's unfair to punish yourself for them. You didn't know back then. I am in no way ashamed of my failures or missteps in my life, as this is what life is all about and no experience is ever wasted. Everything I have done in life: the good, the bad and weird has taught me a lesson, even if it is one that I would not revisit again. As we grow up, we evolve and, in some way, we need to trust the journey, remove our amour and live and love with our whole heart. Just like the ancient Japanese art of Kintsugi, things fall apart. If you are wise, you can use things to patch yourself up and keep going and keep being useful to yourself and others.

Epilogue

Getting older is an extraordinary process as it helps you become the person you should have always been.

I will allow myself to be fully immersed in life and my culture and I finally feel that I can be myself – the talkative, funny, smart, kind hearted, go-getter Australian-Italian Giussa who loves deeply and wants to empower others and experience many opportunities and adventures in life despite her age, gender and background.

There are amazing adventures ahead of me and it is time for me to show up, peel back another layer of myself and step up and help others. It is also time to and live and love with all I have in my heart and soul.

It turns out that the fork in the road and the sign I was looking for upon my dad's passing wasn't a sign after all. I was looking for confirmation of what I already knew. I wanted a nod of approval or a sign that those rules I adhered to led me on the right path in life and that cultural journey made me who I really was. And that is exactly what I found. I hope you enjoyed my book.

Much love and Shining Light

Claudia xx

My parents Luisa and Carmine

My sisters and I, the younger years

My forever chaperone, my sister Diana

Giussa School and University Days

Early Career Days

Adventure Days

Our Wedding Day

Marcus, My Greatest Achievement

Marcus – My Shining Light

Message to My Readers

You are never too old to set another goal or dream a new dream. Connect with others, dream big and live kinder.

Life is a journey, not a destination.

What you think you become, what you feel you attract, what you imagine you create – Buddha

Message to Myself

Take a deep breath and remember who you are. Know your worth because you have greatness within you.

Take a moment and consider where you are right now in your life and how far you have come. I see you. Stand tall and just be you.

Be your own inspiration. Our thoughts create our reality. It is your job to live a life that is authentically yours.

There are unchartered adventures ahead of you. It is time to show up and live and love with your whole heart and soul.

Kiss the faces of your friends; hug their broken pieces back together. Connect with every ounce of who you are, with every inch of your patchwork heart.

To My Father, Carmine

Dear Pa,

Now you are sitting in heaven looking down on all of us and you are no longer sitting on your chair relaxing in the lounge room.

I wanted to tell you that I am enough as I am and I am going to still keep trying to be the best version of myself and live my greatest life, my way.

I've got this Pa; you don't have to worry about me anymore. You did a good job.

I am grateful for all the Italian values you taught me along the way and your hard work and dedication to our family. I will not forget them and will ensure that your grandchild Marcus will remember your journey, all the Italian ways and that your memory will live on through all of us.

Love always your rule breaker, kind, adventurous and ambitious child born in Australia in a drawer.

Ciao, Claudia xo

To My Family

Despite the struggles I have had in defining my path, I am forever grateful to my entire extended family. In particular my immediate family: husband John, my child Marcus, my parents Carmine and Luisa and my sisters Laura, Diana and Celeste. Lots of love also to my brother-in-law's, sister-in-law's, nieces and nephews. I am so grateful for you all in my life. Much love to you all.

To My Friends

A big thank you to all my friends who have helped me during this journey of writing this book and for those who attended my focus groups, participated on my VIP Facebook page and friends that spoke to me personally about their own cultural stories. There have been so many who have helped me feel confident in pursuing this dream of writing my personal story. Thank you to those individuals that personally supported me during my writing meltdowns and periods of self-doubt. I will be forever grateful for your encouragement and support during this time, especially your connections and friendships. I feel very fortunate to have you all in my life.

"**The** *most beautiful things in life are not just things, they are people and moments that make you laugh and smile*".

To My Giussa Girlfriends & Soul Sisters

Thank you soul sisters for the divine connection and embracing life together. I am a better person in this world as a result of all your connections and friendships.

Let's go for it together Giussas, we have the power and strength to achieve anything. Let's not be afraid to be who we really are and let's shine brightly together. Connect with the people who make you feel deeply. Hold them dear, they are your magical people. Connect with the moments that bring tears to your eyes. Just connect: because beautiful things are vanishing each and every day.

We are all essentially a work in progress and I encourage you all to keep learning, keep growing and keep dreaming.

Don't worry how long it takes, just focus on taking that first step and you will get there. One day you will look back and you will be proud and happy that you took a chance and that you ended up achieving what you had set out to do. It's better to look back in life and say look at what I have achieved or tried something than to look back and say "I wish I had done that". Eventually we all end up where we need to be in life.

May we always remember to support each other in good and in the hard times. Always remember to be kind to yourself and others.

Let's release all the narratives in our lives that no longer serve us and embrace change and express our true selves.

Always remember as Walt Disney said - "If you can dream it, you can do it".

Message to My Publishing Coach

Thankyou Emma Hamlin for believing in me, and helping me reach another bucket list dream: helping me to publish my very own solo book. You are truly a magical Change Maker, and our very own Wizard of Oz.

You've always had the power my dear, you just had to learn it for yourself – the Wizard of Oz.

Message to My Editor

Thankyou to my beautiful mum friend and talented editor, Kate Boccaccio. I will be forever grateful for your constant support, guidance and help in the process of editing this book. We may have found each other through our children's primary school, but our soul sister connection will last forever.

A Letter to My Only Child, Marcus

I am writing this letter to you as a reminder of how wonderful and beautiful you are and to tell you that when you came into this world, you brought love into my heart and soul that I had never experienced.

When I look into your eyes I am so proud of the person you are and what you are capable of still becoming. You have such a kind nature and beautiful soul and I am lucky to have you as my only child.

Life will have its ups and downs and this will challenge you throughout your life, but I know your strength and resilience will see you through. Remember it is not about the failure in our life that defines us, but the moments when we decide to get back up and try again.

Enjoy the adventures of being young and try to make time to enjoy new experiences, learn new things and most importantly, simply to have fun and connect with others. Don't be afraid to take risks and reach beyond your comfort zone and expand your horizons. Become the leader of your own life. Be brave, courageous and dream big.

Live your own dreams. Find out what makes you truly happy and pursue it. Follow your own path in life. Live your life with a purpose. Be kind, humble, respectful, and loving to yourself and others always. Choose to be kind over being right, because kindness is a sign of strength.

Never feel the need to listen to someone who wants to define you. Keep strong and keep trying to improve yourself to be the best version of you. Son, you alone hold the power. You have all the power within yourself to manifest your dreams. Be true to yourself always and allow your uniqueness to shine through. Do not be afraid to be who you really are. You are enough as you are.

Your worth is what shines from your eyes when you laugh and smile and be your true authentic self. Speak your truth, share your soul and connect with others.

We don't know what tomorrow will bring so it is important to be thankful for another day. Learn to forgive and love with all your heart and enjoy the people that love you. Keep being someone's light when they are hopeless, just like you were mine.

You are my Shining Light in this world and I will be forever grateful for your constant toddler laughs and smiles that pulled me away from my darkness and allowed the light to shine in my world again.

I love you to the moon and back.

Big hugs, Love you always and forever.

Mum x

About the Author

Born in Adelaide, Australia, to Italian immigrant parents, Claudia Callisto is an Amazon bestselling author and the co-founder of Shining Light, an organisation that provides women and children the tools to practice mindfulness, kindness and gratitude, as well as develop positive mindsets.

Claudia is a wife and a mother to one child, Marcus. She is a passionate amateur photographer and loves ticking things off her bucket list. Claudia also loves spending time with her family and friends laughing, eating, and preparing rustic food to enjoy together.